At Home with PHONICS

Grade 2

Fun Activities, Games, and Puzzles

STECK-VAUGHN
A Harcourt Company

www.svschoolsupply.com
www.rigby.com

Core Skills Workbooks
Titles You Can Trust

The education of our children is a matter of trust not entered into lightly. Steck-Vaughn shares an ongoing partnership with today's schools and educational programs, committed to providing young learners with opportunities to enrich and expand their educational horizons.

Steck-Vaughn School Supply's Core Skills series offers parents and educators high-quality, curriculum-based products that reflect the concepts and skills outlined in national standards. The content of these programs has proven successful in classroom environments, and now we are bringing that content home to you. We are delighted that you have extended your trust to us. Welcome to the partnership of the publisher, the school, and parents—on behalf of our children.

For more information on Steck-Vaughn School Supply, please visit our website at www.svschoolsupply.com

Editors: Carol Allison and Mary Susnis
Executive Editor: Georgine Cooper
Design Production Manager: Tom Sjoerdsma
Interior Design Support: Noel Arreola
Cover Design: Phil Meilinger
Cover Photography: Brian Warling

Text and illustrations copyright ©2004 Steck-Vaughn.
Printed in the United States of America.
All Rights Reserved.

09 08 07 06 05 04
10 9 8 7 6 5 4 3 2 1

ISBN 0–7398–7957–X
At Home with Phonics: Fun Activities, Games, and Puzzles

This book is intended for classroom or at-home use and not for resale or distribution and may not be reproduced without permission in writing from the publisher. Inquiries should be addressed to: Copyright Permissions, Steck-Vaughn Company, P.O. Box 26015, Austin, TX 78755.

Table of Contents

5-6	Introduction

Part I — Vowels and Vowel Patterns

7	Parent Pointers
8-10	Short a, i, and u
11-12	Short e and o
13-14	Long vowels: *CVCe*
15-16	Long a: *ai, ay*
17-18	Long e: *Ce, y, ey*
19-20	Long e: *ea, ee*
21-22	Long e: *ei, ie*
23-24	Long i: *Cie, Cy, CCy*
25-26	Long o: *Co, ow*
27-28	Long o: *oa*
29-30	Long i: *igh*
31-32	Long a: *eigh*
33-34	Sound of *au* and *aw*
35-36	Sound of *ea* in *head*
37-39	Sound of *ou* and *ow* in *house* and *how*
40-41	Sound of *oi* and *oy*
42-43	Sound of *oo* and *ou* in *took* and *would*
44-45	Sound of *ou* in *touch*
46-47	Sound of *ew* and *ue* in *new* and *blue*
48-49	Sound of *a* and *al* in *water* and *walk*
50-52	R-Controlled Vowels: *er, ir, ur, ear*
53-54	R-Controlled Vowels: *ear, eer, /ir/*
55	R-Controlled Vowel: *ar*
56-58	R-Controlled Vowel: *or, ore*
59-60	R-Controlled Vowels: *oar, oor, our*
61-63	R-Controlled Vowels: *air, are, ear*
64	Single Long Vowels

Part II — Medial and Silent Consonants, Consonant Blends, and Digraphs

65	Parent Pointers
66-67	Medial Consonants
68-70	Silent Consonants: *dge, kn, wr*
71-73	Initial 2-Letter Consonant Blends
74-75	Initial 3-Letter Consonant Blends
76	Final Consonant Blends: *ft, ld, lt, nt*
77-78	Final Consonant Blends: *mp, nd, sk, st*
79-80	Initial Consonant Digraphs: *ch, sh, th, wh*
81-84	Final Consonant Digraphs: *ch, sh, tch, th*
85-86	Final Consonant Digraphs: *ck, ng, nk*
87-88	Consonant Digraphs: *gh, ph /f/*

At Home with Phonics

Part III	Verb Endings, Plural Endings and Comparative Endings
89	Parent Pointers
90–92	Action Word Ending *ed*
93–97	Action Word Endings *ed, ing*
98–104	Action Word Endings *es, ing, s*
105–108	Plural Endings *s, es*
109–110	Plural Ending *es*
111–112	Comparative Endings *er, est*

Part IV	Suffixes, Prefixes, Contractions, Compound Words, and Possessives
113	Parent Pointers
114–115	Suffixes *ful, y*
116–117	Suffix *ly*
118–119	Suffix *ness*
120–121	Suffix *able*
122–124	Prefixes *dis, un*
125–127	Prefixes *pre, re*
128–130	Contractions with *'d, 're, 've*
131–133	Contractions with *'ll, 'm, n't, 's*
134–136	Compound Words
137–138	Singular and Plural Possessives
139–140	Answer Key
141	Phonics Skills Checklist
142–143	Progress Chart
144	Photo Acknowledgements

Grade 2 Benchmarks

Benchmarks are standards of achievement. The following are grade two benchmarks. Do not expect that all children will have achieved these benchmarks. Benchmarks are used to guide further practice and to measure progress. At the end of second grade, your child may demonstrate the ability to...

- hear and isolate beginning, middle, and final sounds.
- use mostly conventional spelling or know how to correct spellings.
- use word families to figure out unknown words, for example, -an, -est, -ing, -ore.
- use clues within the text to find meaning. *Does the word look right? Does it sound right? Does this make sense?*
- identify short and long vowel sounds.

Core Skills

Introduction

At Home with Phonics: Fun Activities, Games, and Puzzles provides enjoyable practice in grade level phonics skills for your child. Activities are grouped by skill and can be used in any order.

Partner Icon

Literacy skills develop over time through a variety of literacy experiences. Some children may require support to be able to complete these phonics activities. You may provide support by reading aloud, talking about the pictures, or helping with the writing. Most activities are designed for individual practice. Partner or family activities are identified by the *Partner Icon*.

Each section of *At Home with Phonics* includes Parent Pointers that list the skills practiced, extension activities, and website resources. Post the Progress Chart (pages 142-143) to help you keep track of phonics practice. Use the tear-out Answer Key and Phonics Skills Checklist to evaluate your child's progress.

Phonics Q & A

How can **At Home with Phonics** *help my child?*
- Engaging activities provide phonics practice to help your child achieve reading success and build confidence.
- Meaningful reading and writing experiences invite children to apply knowledge of sounds, letters, and words.
- Puzzles and games allow children to share the joy of reading success.
- Easy-to-use teaching strategies and tools help parents gain confidence as their children's first teachers.
- Parent Pointers extend classroom phonics skills into practical at-home fun.

How does phonics help my child with reading and writing?
Phonics activities…
- build on your child's connections between letters and sounds.
- are an important *part* of learning to read and write.
- help your child learn to recognize words automatically.

What can I do to help my child become a better reader and writer?
One of the most important ways you can help your child with reading and writing is to watch and listen to how your child uses language. The following suggestions can help you get started:
- Engage your child in meaningful conversation, showing the give and take of conversation. Help your child see the connections between listening, speaking, reading, and writing.
- Have fun with words by making rhymes, clapping syllables, and listening for beginning or ending sounds.
- Model reading and talk about it with your child. When your child observes you reading, he or she learns that reading is important.
- Read and reread many kinds of books aloud to your child.
- Listen to recordings of stories, songs, or rhymes.

- Share-read a familiar book, poem, rhyme or song. A very young child can memorize familiar stories and rhymes and "pretend read" with you.
- Play with magnetic alphabet letters to form words. Sort words, letters, or sounds.
- Observe letters and words on billboards, signs, menus, labels, cereal boxes, and so on.
- Ask your child to help you with everyday writing. Make a shopping list, a card, a holiday letter, a sign, or a thank you note. Let your child "invent" a spelling that makes sense if he or she is unsure of how to spell a word.
- As your child tells a story, offer to write the captions or title.

I am not a teacher; how do I help my child learn?
- Observe and listen to find out what your child already knows, what is confusing, and what he or she wants to learn.
- Allow your child the time to practice and the freedom to make mistakes.
- Follow these four steps of teaching and learning:
  Step 1: Show your child how. Say, *I'll do; you watch.*
  Step 2: Let your child help. Say, *I'll do; you help.*
  Step 3: Let your child practice. Say, *You do; I'll help.*
  Step 4: Let your child show what he or she has learned.
  Say, *You do; I'll watch.*

A Parent's Dictionary of Phonics Terms

Phonics is the understanding that there is a connection between the sounds of spoken language (phonemes) and the letters that represent the sounds (graphemes).

Sound Symbol are sounds of letter(s) indicated by the symbol of a letter(s) enclosed in backslashes /a/, /ch/, /ks/.

Vowels are the letters *a, e, i, o, u* and sometimes *y*. The sounds of vowels can be *short* (the /a/ as in *cat*) or *long* (the /a/ in *cape*) when the vowel letter "says its name."

R-Controlled Vowels are vowel letters that produce a distinct sound because they are followed by the letter r, such as *ar, er, ir, ur*.

Consonants are the letters of the alphabet that are not vowels.

Consonant Blends are consonant letters that blend their sounds together, but both sounds can still be identified. For example, *pl, cr,* or *sw,* or *str*.

Consonant Digraphs are consonant letters that "work together like partners" to create one new sound. For example, *th, ch, sh*.

Suffixes are word parts that are attached to the end of a root word or base word to form a new word. For example, *slow + ly = slowly*.

Prefixes are word parts that are attached to the beginning of a root word or base word to form a new word. For example, *pre + view = preview*.

Compound Words are words formed by putting together two or more smaller words. For example, *cup + cake = cupcake*

Contractions are shortened forms of words formed by omitting a letter (or letters) and replacing it with an apostrophe. For example, *could not = couldn't*.

Possessives are forms of words that show ownership by adding 's or s' to a noun. For example, *The coat that belongs to Sam is Sam's coat. Toys that belong to the twins are the twins' toys.*

Part 1: Vowels and Vowel Patterns

★ Parent Pointers

Skills Short Vowels Review • Long Vowel Patterns • Long and Short Vowel Combinations • R-Controlled Vowels

Extension Activities

Word Ladders
Draw a ladder with several rungs on a sheet of paper or on an erasable board. Write a long vowel phonogram, such as *ake*, at the top of the ladder. Encourage your child to fill the ladder rungs with words that fit the pattern, such as *take, cake, make, wake, rake*. Continue by drawing ladders for other long vowel patterns, such as *ace, ade, age, ale, ane, ame, ate*. Change the vowel sound to build other word ladders.

Skill: Long Vowel Patterns

Yarn Words
Give your child a length of yarn. Say the word *yarn* and listen to the vowel sound. Ask your child to make the letters of a word with the same vowel-r sound as *yarn*. Have your child cut the yarn to form the letters and paste the letters on a heavy sheet of paper. Then ask your child to draw a picture to illustrate the word. Display the yarn word and the drawing.

Skill: R-Controlled Vowels

Word Riddles
Have your child search a book for all the *er, ir, ur,* and *ear* words he or she can find and list the words. Invite your child to make a riddle for each of the words. Have the child write the riddle on one side of an index card and the answer on the other. Plan time to allow your child to challenge other members of the family to guess his or her riddles.

Skill: R-Controlled Vowels

Website Resources
National Education Association
Parent Resources
http://www.nea.org

Steck-Vaughn is not responsible for the content of any website listed here. All material is the responsibility of the hosts and creators.

At Home with Phonics 7

Pets on Parade

mud	pin	pack
tub	hid	fun
it	bat	an

- Read and say the words in the list.
- Write the words that match the vowel sound in the middle of each animal's name.
- Write other words that have the same sounds.

Short a, i, and u

Rhyme Time

- Read the words on each fish aloud.
- Color the parts that have rhyming words the same.

Fish 1: Jack, sick, sack
Fish 2: pat, pan, in, pin
Fish 3: back, pig, wig, big
Fish 4: hit, fat, run, fun
Fish 5: tin, lip, tip, tan
Fish 6: map, cap, cat
Fish 7: rub, tab, rib, tub
Fish 8: bug, run, rug, bag

Short a, i, and u 9

Puzzle Page

- Write the letter that begins the word for each picture.
- Read the words you make.

1. 🥫 + ☂ + 🐷 = ◯ __ __ __

2. 🐷 + 🍎 + 🌰 = __ ◯ __

3. ❤ + 🍎 + 🐢 = __ __ ◯

- Use the letters in the circles to answer this question.

  ____ ____ ____

- Make some puzzles of your own.

What do I think is the best pet?

10 Short a, i, and u

Catch the Birds

Oh, no! The birds got out!

- Read the words on the birds.
- Then read the hint on each cage.
- Write each word to match.

bed

rock

mess

top

1. A frog likes to sit on this.
   _____

2. You can play with this.
   _____

3. You can nap in this.
   _____

4. You may get this if you spill.
   _____

Short e and o

Silly Pets

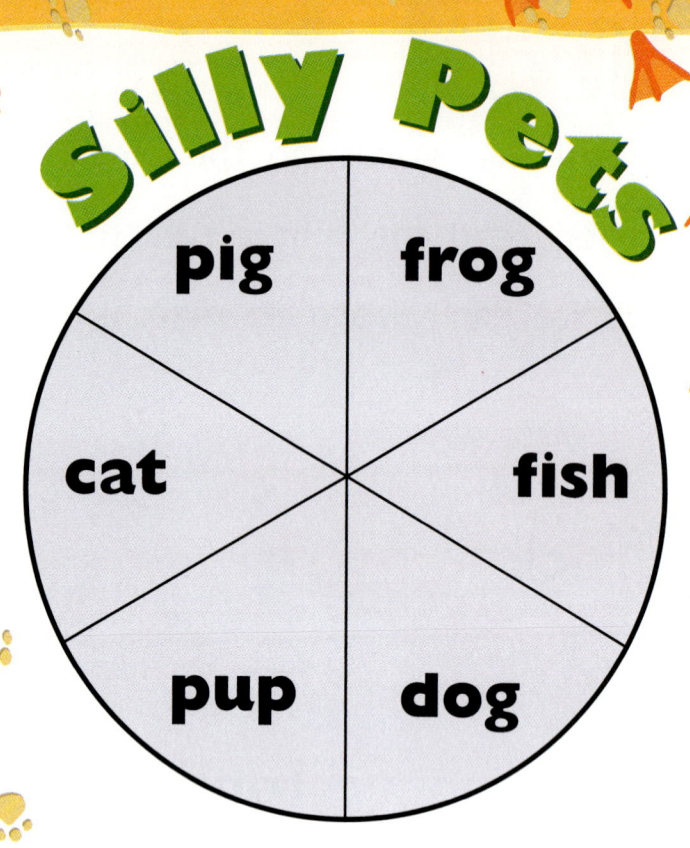

Wheel 1: pig, frog, fish, dog, pup, cat

- Read the word wheels.

- Shut your eyes and move a finger around each wheel. Look and write the word from each wheel that you stop on.

I see a _____

with a _____.

I see a _____

with a _____.

I see a _____

with a _____.

Wheel 2: hat, net, pen, mop, dress, wig

- Draw silly pictures for your writing.

12 Short e and o

Find a Rhyme

gate bike
fuse tape
time fine
broke tone

- Write a list word that rhymes.

1. lime _____   **2.** mine _____

3. spoke _____   **4.** cape _____

5. bone _____   **6.** hike _____

7. use _____   **8.** late _____

- Say and connect the dots for answers 1 to 8.

What toy is this?

_____

Long vowels: CVCe   13

Word Hunt

Some kids hid their toys.
They wrote a note in code.
Can you crack the code?

- Read the note.

P-s-s-s-t! Cross out each of these letters: g h v x

Hello. These are the toys we hid.

g a x b a k e v h s e t g h v x
x v a g r e d h k i t e v x g h
g h x h a h c u t e v d o l l g
x a g j u m p h r o p e v x g x
a g l i t t l e v b i k e h x v

- Draw the missing toys.

14 Long vowels: CVCe

What Is It?

Gail and Ray are two friends. What do they like to do?

- Read all the words aloud.
- Color each box that has a word with a **long a** sound.

Find a surprise word!

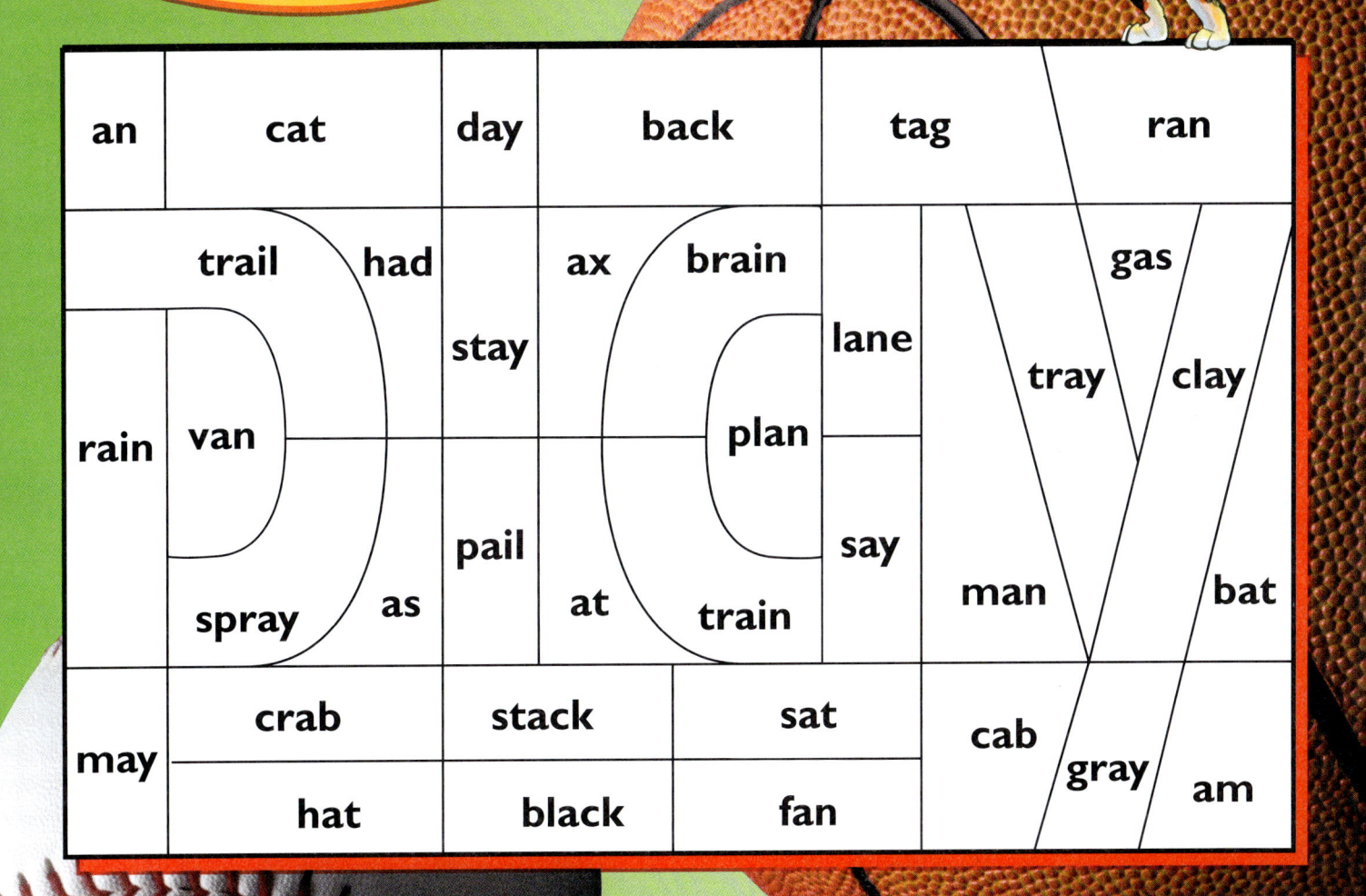

an	cat	day	back	tag	ran
rain	trail	had	ax	brain	gas
	van	stay		lane	tray	clay
			plan			
	spray	as	pail	at	say	man	bat
				train			
may	crab	stack	sat	cab	gray	am
	hat	black	fan			

Long a: *ai, ay*

On Rainy Days

What do you do when it rains? Do you like to play inside? It is fun to make things. You may make a clay pot. You may paint a snake.

What games do you like to play? Sometimes it is fun to make up games. What game could you play with a ball and a pail? What game could you play with tape and a paper tail?

Rainy days can be fun. You just have to use your brain!

Read the questions. Answer **yes** or **no.**

- Do you like to play inside? _____

- Do you like to make things? _____

- Have you ever made up a game? _____

• Write about a game with a ball and a pail.

_____

_____

Long a: *ai, ay*

The Lost Key

- Draw what is in the safe.

Tommy is not happy.

He lost the key to his safe.

There are twenty dimes in the safe.

There is a penny, too.

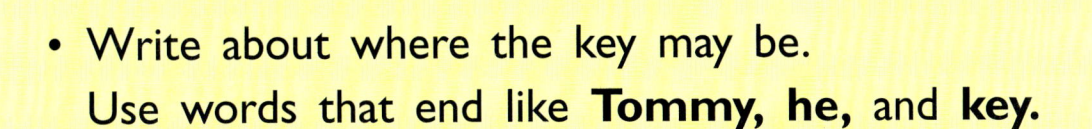

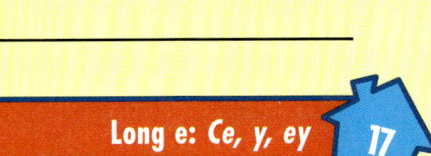

- Write about where the key may be. Use words that end like **Tommy, he,** and **key.**

_____

_____

Long e: Ce, y, ey 17

Empty the Piggy

Sometimes **y** sounds like **e**.

- Each number stands for a letter.
- Use the code's key to write a letter in each blank.
- Read out loud.

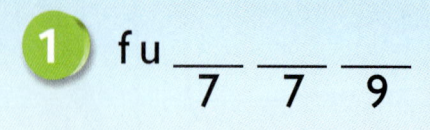

a	e	g	h	l	m	n	p	y
1	2	3	4	5	6	7	8	9

1 f u __ __ __
       7 7 9

2 __ __
      6 2

3 __ i __ __ __
      8   3 3 9

4 __ __ __ __ __
      4 1 8 8 9

5 __ __ __ t __
      2 6 8   9

6 __ __
      4 2

7 __ o __ __ __
      6   7 2 9

8 v __ __ __ __ __
        1 5 5 2 9

Long e: Ce, y, ey

Fast Feet

Jean needs to get to the bank.

She will take the streets with words that have the same **e** sound as **feet.**

- Read each word.
- Draw a line to show Jean the way.

eat

desk   neck   rest   green   creep

get   see

mend

meal   crest   smell

bean   pet

heat   jeep   queen

cent

Long e: *ea, ee*   19

Treasure Hunt

Dean hid some money.
Will it be easy to find?
- Read the directions.
- Draw footprints to show the way to the money.

1. Begin at the tree.
2. Go up and down the steep hill.
3. Go over the stream.
4. Go to the green rock.
5. Peek in the tent.

Where did Dean hide the money?

_____
_____

Long e: *ea, ee*

What Is Missing?

Neil has a wish.
He is out in the field.
Sheila hits the ball.
Neil holds up his mitt.
What a relief!
Does Neil get his wish?

- Draw what is missing.
- Write words with **ei** and **ie**.

_____

_____

_____

_____

Long e: *ei, ie*

Word Hunt

- Color the letter in the first box.
- Skip a box and color the next box.
- Keep going—skip a box and color a box.

Dear Tommie,
I need your help to

m	s	b	e	j	i	p	z	k
e	r	t	h	h	w	e	l	t
z	h	o	i	s	e	m	f	n

Chief Shield

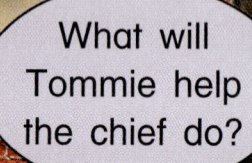

What will Tommie help the chief do?

Write the letters that are left to find out.

__ __ __ __ __   __ __ __   __ __ __ __ __

22 Long e: *ei* and *ie*

A Game for One

Ty wants a kite. Cy wants a ball.

- Play tic tac toe by yourself.
- Make ◇'s for Ty and ○'s for Cy instead of **X**'s and **O**'s.

The boy who wins will get his wish.

1. Put a kite on **lie**.
2. Put a ball on **dry**.
3. Put a kite on **try**.
4. Put a ball on **why**.
5. Put a kite on **my**.
6. Put a ball on **pie**.
7. Put a kite on **fly**.
8. Put a ball on **by**.

tie	my	fly
why	try	lie
by	dry	pie

Who will get his wish?

Long i: Cie, Cy, CCy

Dream On

- Color the letters with words that have the **long i** sound spelled **ie** as in **tie** or **y** as in **my**.

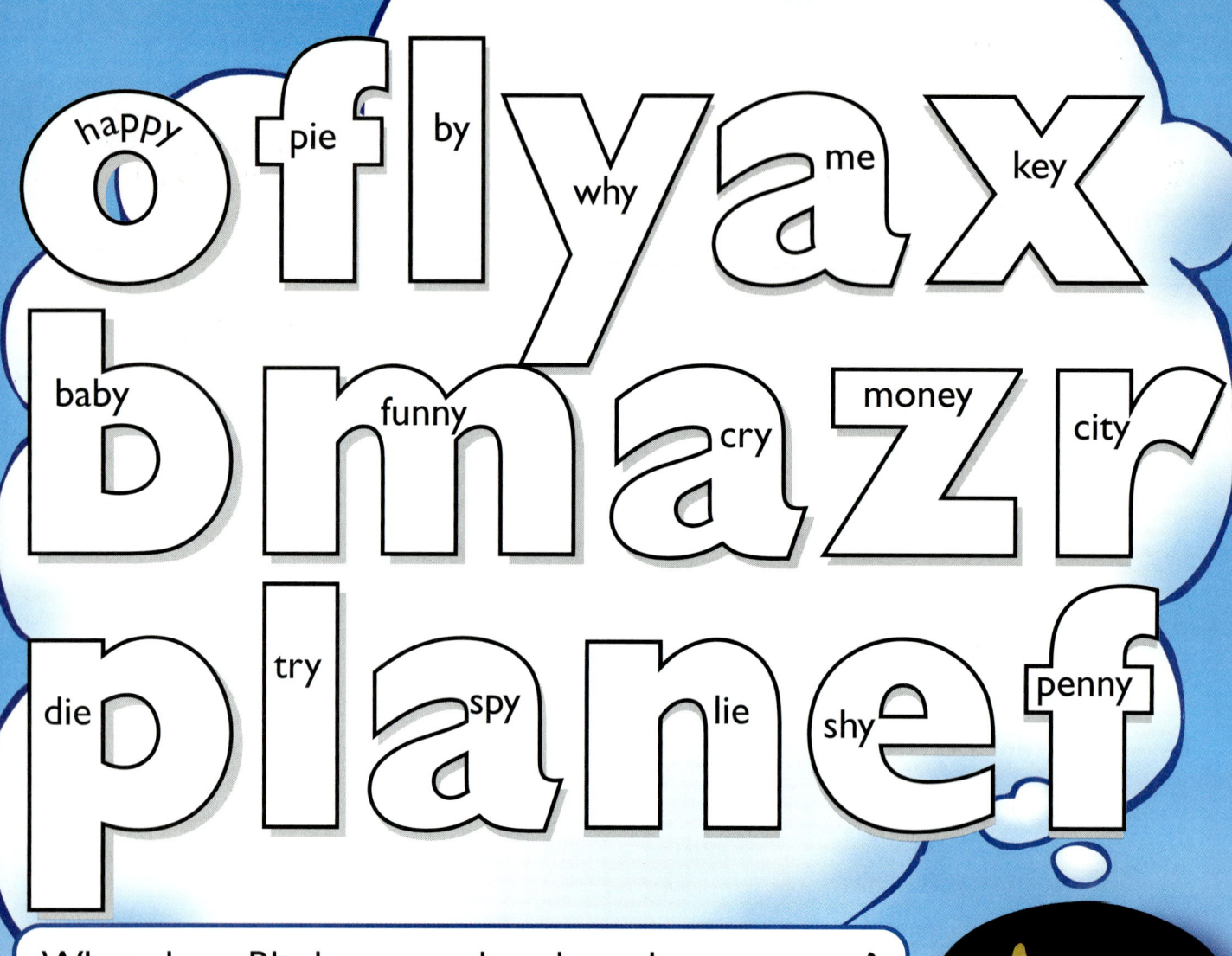

Letters with words:
- o — happy
- f — pie
- l — by
- y — why
- a — me
- x — key
- b — baby
- m — funny
- a — cry
- z — money
- r — city
- p — die
- l — try
- a — spy
- n — lie
- e — shy
- f — penny

What does Bly hope to do when she grows up?
_____

24 Long i: Cie, Cy, CCy

What Number Are You Calling?

- Read the clues.
- Use letters on the buttons to make words with **long o** as in **grow**.
- Write the words on the lines.

Clues

1. You can make this with ribbon. ___ ___ ___

2. The wind can do this. ___ ___ ___ ___

3. You can do this with a ball. ___ ___ ___ ___ ___

4. It is white and cold. ___ ___ ___ ___

5. It is black and can fly. ___ ___ ___ ___

6. It means **not high**. ___ ___ ___

Long o: Co, ow 25

It's in the Mail

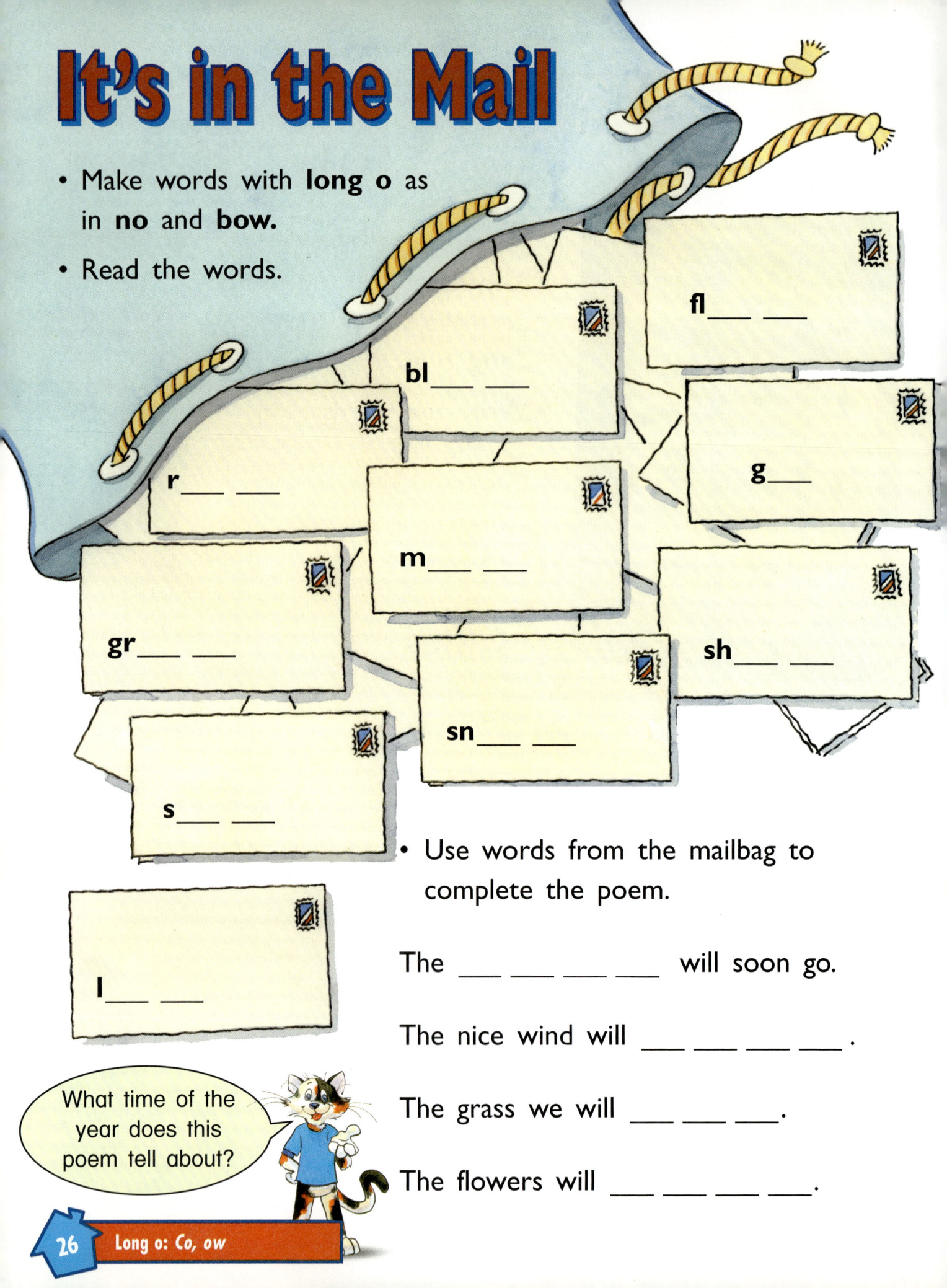

- Make words with **long o** as in **no** and **bow**.
- Read the words.

fl___ ___

bl___ ___

g___

r___ ___

m___ ___

gr___ ___

sh___ ___

sn___ ___

s___ ___

l___ ___

- Use words from the mailbag to complete the poem.

The ___ ___ ___ ___ will soon go.

The nice wind will ___ ___ ___ ___.

The grass we will ___ ___ ___.

The flowers will ___ ___ ___ ___.

What time of the year does this poem tell about?

26 Long o: Co, ow

Word Hunt

- Read the clues.
- Find and circle each answer in the puzzle. Words can go →, ↓, or ↘.

Each word has **oa**.

Clues

1. Mom drives the van on this.
2. A ship can do this.
3. You might eat this with jam.
4. This makes you clean.
5. A frog can do this.
6. This means to get wet.
7. You can float in this.
8. This looks like a frog.

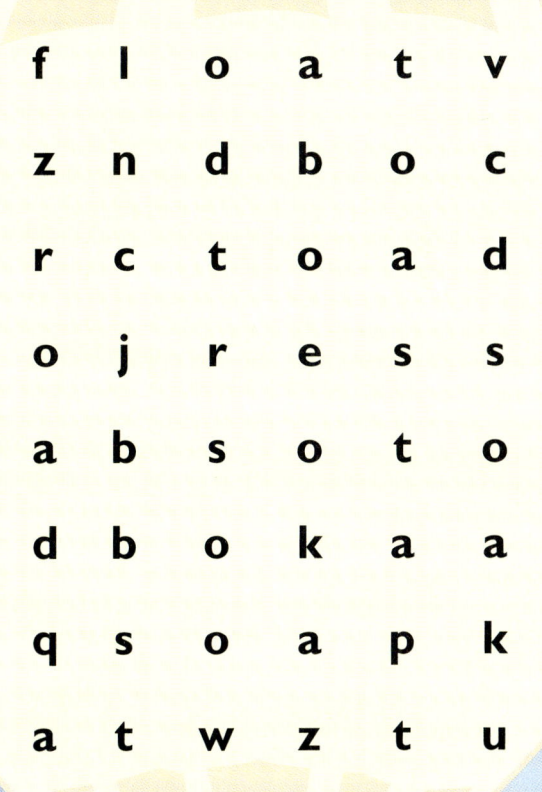

f	l	o	a	t	v
z	n	d	b	o	c
r	c	t	o	a	d
o	j	r	e	s	s
a	b	s	o	t	o
d	b	o	k	a	a
q	s	o	a	p	k
a	t	w	z	t	u

Long o: *oa* 27

Puzzle Page

Each word has **igh**.

- Write the missing words for the clues.
- Write the missing clues for the words.

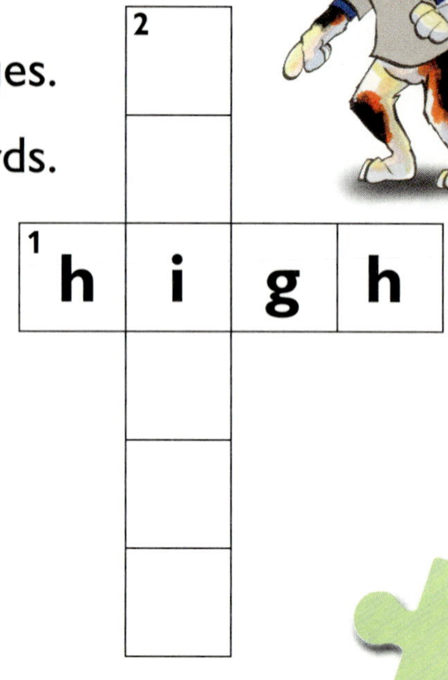
2
1 h i g h

1. ______________ ______________

2. a plane trip

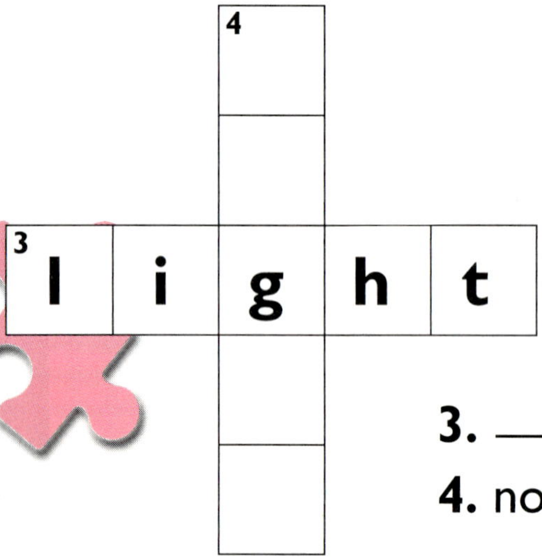
4
3 l i g h t

3. ______________ ______________

4. not day

5. ______________ ______________

6. means **may**

6
5 r i g h t

Puzzle Page

All the words have the **a** sound spelled **eigh.**

Clues

1. What can you ride in the snow?
2. What number comes after seventeen?
3. What word means **how heavy a thing is?**
4. What do you call someone who lives next door?
5. How many legs does a spider have?
6. What does a horse say?

Long a: *eigh*

Snowy Days

- Color the shapes whose numbers have the sound of **a** as in **weigh**.

47, 64, 2, 95, 105, 24, 45, 25, 76, 56, 39, 79, 4, 82, 48, 80, 31, 3, 18, 86, 78, 12, 58, 70, 15, 72, 38, 20, 43, 28, 108, 1, 8, 98, 68, 7, 6, 71, 26, 13, 91, 23, 61, 14, 9

- What is hidden in the spaces? _____

32 Long a: *eigh*

What Is Missing?

Have you seen my neighbor, Mrs. August? You can see her driving around town in a yellow auto with a claw painted on each side. She hauls straw for her pet ducks in the back seat. There is also a pail for the fish she has caught. Sometimes on chilly fall days, she wears a shawl.

- Draw what is missing!

Sound of *au* and *aw*

Awesome Words

- Write **au** or **aw** to finish each word. Use the code to help.

The letters **au** and **aw** sound the same in these words.

au 🛼 **aw** 🏈

th___ ___ (aw)   h___ ___k (aw)   p___ ___se (au)   str___ ___ (aw)

f___ ___n (aw)   h___ ___l (au)   p___ ___ (aw)   t___ ___ght (au)

- Write each word by its meaning

1. a large bird _____   2. stop for a bit _____

3. melt _____   4. a baby deer _____

5. animal foot _____   6. move or pull _____

7. helped learn _____   8. dry grass _____

Sound of *au* and *aw*

Jake likes to help his mom get lunch ready.
- Read the clues.
- Use the letters to write words that have the sound of **ea** as in **head.**

Time for Lunch

1. You put your hat on this. ___ ___ ___ ___
2. This is good with jam. ___ ___ ___ ___
3. Big rocks are this. ___ ___ ___ ___ ___
4. This is a kind of thin string. ___ ___ ___ ___ ___
5. You may do this when you are hot. ___ ___ ___ ___ ___

Clues

Sound of *ea* in *head*

Time Trials

- Read what Kevin wrote.
- Write the words with the sound of **ea** as in **head**.

Get ready... get set...

May 1

I was ready for the race. I had my lucky band on my head.

The race began. I was ahead. Then I started to sweat. My legs felt heavy. I was out of breath.

My time was good, but I did not win. Next time, I will run at a steady pace.

_____

_____

_____

_____

_____

_____

Sound of *ea* in *head*

Perfect Timing

- Get a watch or clock with a second hand. Have a partner use it to time you.
- Read the chart. Answer the questions.
- Write the words you read that have **ou** and **ow** as in **house** and **now**.

Time It	Answer	Words
1. Pout for 10 seconds. Did you do it?		_____
2. Look down for 15 seconds. Did you do it?		_____
3. Count out loud for 20 seconds. How far did you get?		_____ _____ _____ _____
4. Frown for 10 seconds. Did you do it?		_____
5. Do not make a sound. Did you do it for 60 seconds?		_____

Sound of *ou* and *ow* in *house* and *how*

Watch It!

- Read the words aloud.
- Find sections with words that have the sound of **ou** and **ow** in **house** and **how.** Color them brown.
- Color all other sections yellow.

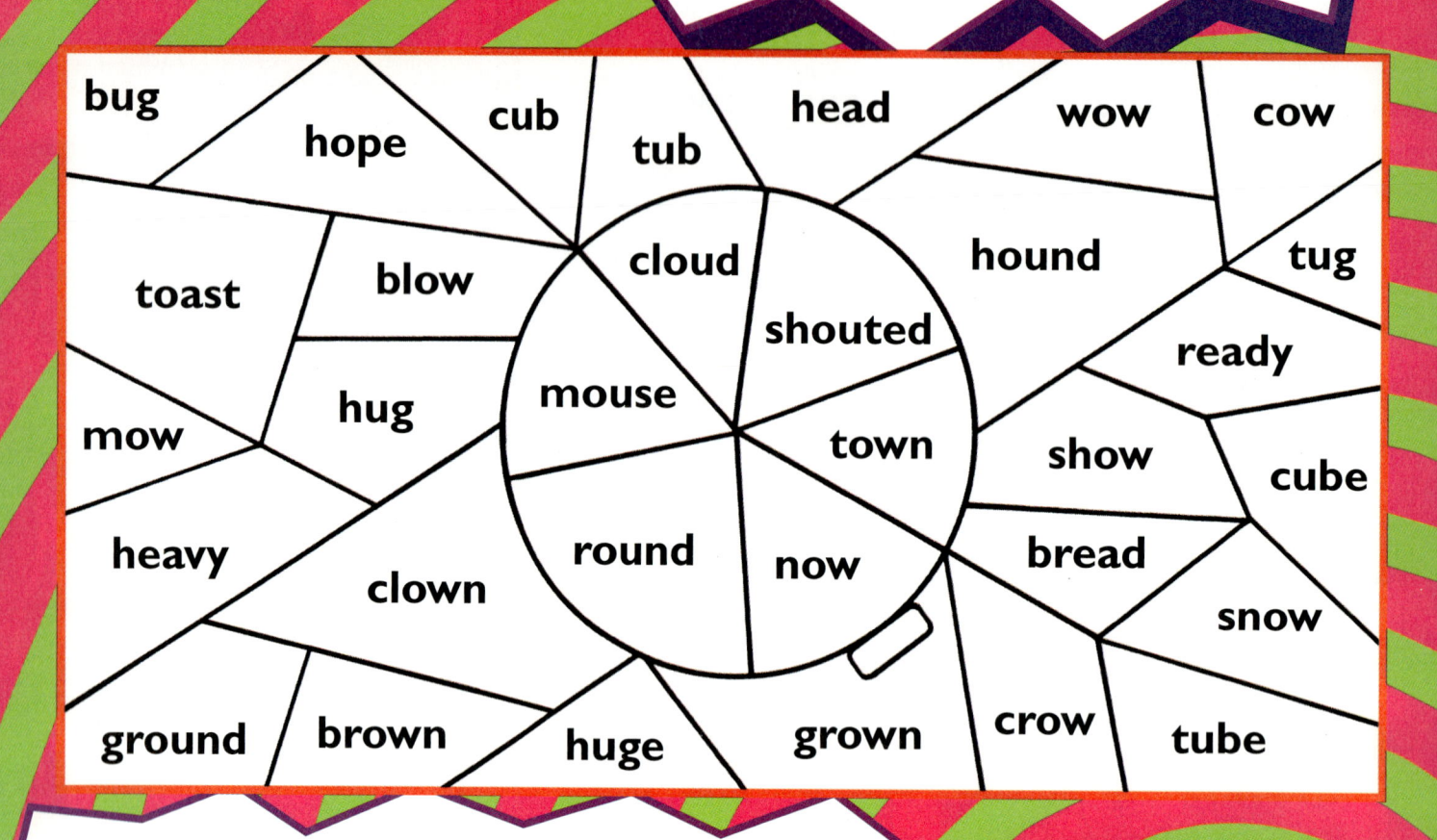

bug, hope, cub, head, wow, cow, tub, toast, blow, cloud, hound, tug, shouted, ready, hug, mouse, town, show, cube, mow, heavy, round, now, bread, snow, clown, ground, brown, huge, grown, crow, tube

- Write **ou** and **ow** to complete this story.

Tom saw something on the gr___ ___nd. It had a r___ ___nd face. It had a br___ ___n band. He picked it up and w___ ___nd it.

"W___ ___!" he sh___ ___ted.

What do you think Tom found?

38 Sound of *ou* and *ow* in *house* and *how*

Word Hunt

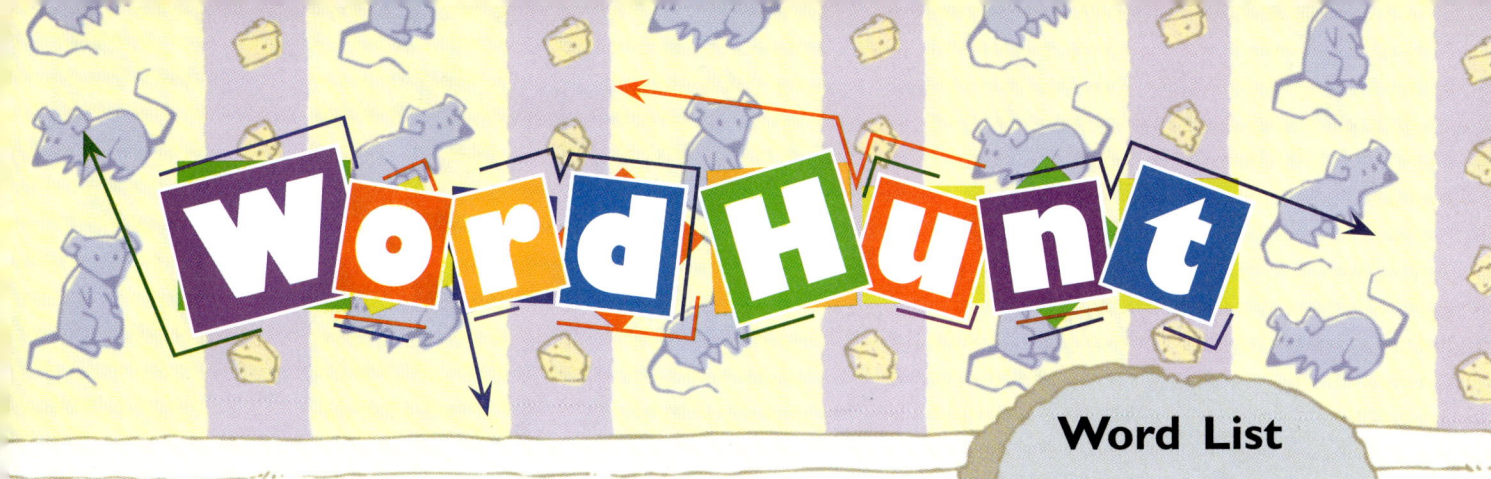

Word List
- found
- house
- mouth
- frown
- down
- count
- clown
- brow

- Read the words in the list.
- Cross out each word in the puzzle.

```
f o u n d m o
r h o u s e m
o d o w n u o
w c l o w n u
n s b r o w t
c o u n t e h
```

- Write the letters you have left to find the answer.

When is it a bad time to be followed by a cat?

when you are a ___ ___ ___ ___ ___

Sound of *ou* and *ow* in *house* and *how* 39

Tic Tac Surprise!

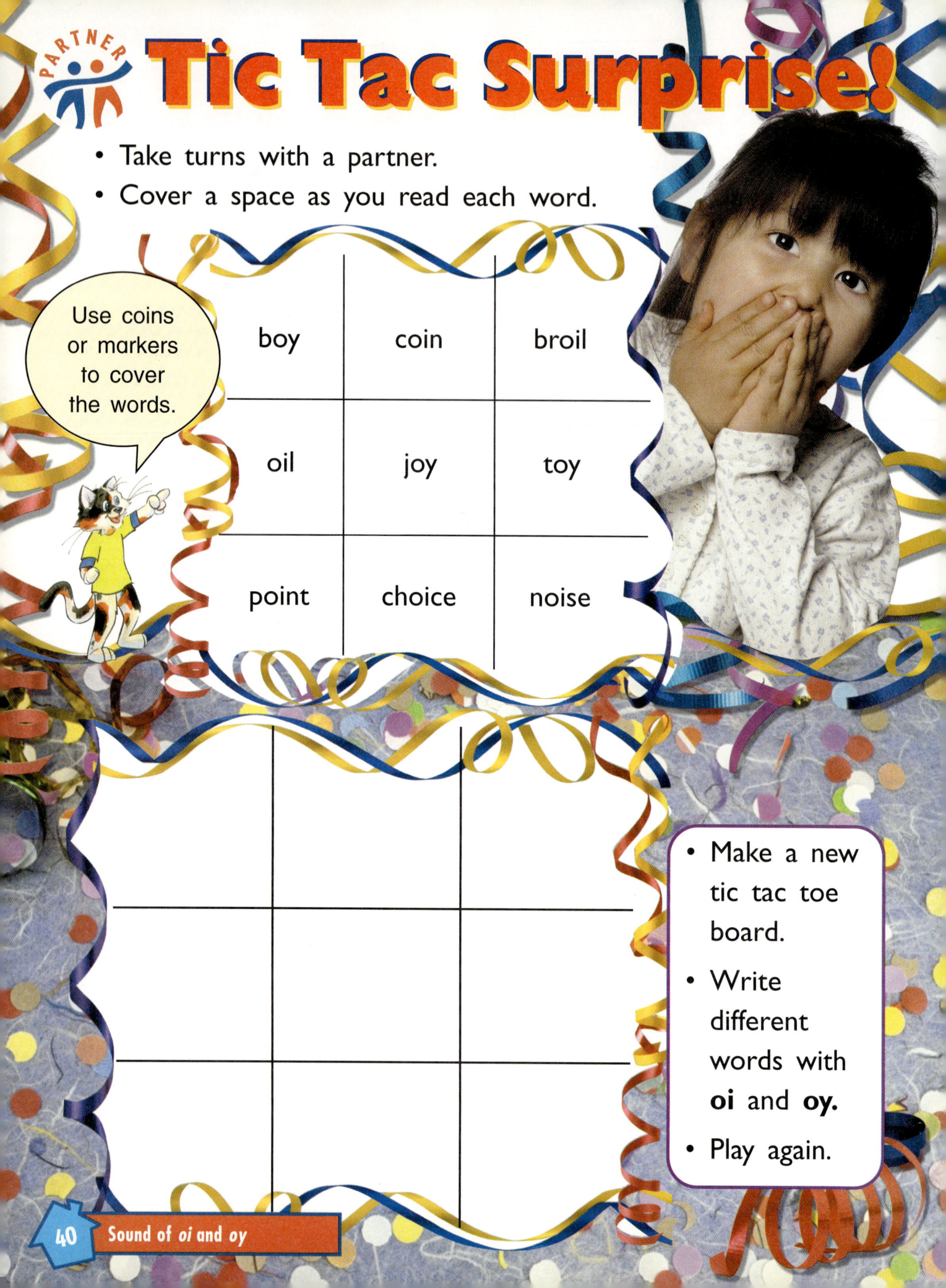

- Take turns with a partner.
- Cover a space as you read each word.

Use coins or markers to cover the words.

boy	coin	broil
oil	joy	toy
point	choice	noise

- Make a new tic tac toe board.
- Write different words with **oi** and **oy**.
- Play again.

Sound of *oi* and *oy*

How on Earth?

Would you like to be a **magician**? Magicians are people who can do tricks.

They may seem to pluck a coin out of the air. They may point to a toy and seem to make it vanish. They may seem to change one rabbit into three.

Magicians need to enjoy acting. They must know how to get you to listen to their voice and not watch their hands.

If you know how to do a trick, do not spoil it for other boys and girls. Let them enjoy the fun!

- Write about a magician's trick. Use words with **oi** or **oy**.
- Draw a picture showing your trick.

Sound of *oi* and *oy*

Say "Cheese"

Miss Wood took a picture of the class. She hoped it would be good.

- Follow the arrows from box to box.
- Write the same letter in each connected box. Some letters are already there.
- Read what Miss Wood said to the class.

Y o u   s h o u l d

l o o k   a t   u s

o n   s m i l e.

Sound of *oo* and *ou* in *took* and *would*

Put It in Writing!

- Write about each picture.
- Use words from the list.

good   book
stood   brook
cook   could
look   should

Sound of *oo* and *ou* in *took* and *would*   43

Fingerprint Clues

When you touch a hard, smooth object, you leave behind fingerprints. Each person's prints are different from anyone else's.

Fingerprints are clues that can help solve tough cases.

double loop

whorl

tented arch

arch

loop

- Use these clues to unscramble the letters.

1. bumpy; not smooth   **ughro**   _____

2. strong; not tender   **houtg**   _____

3. not old   **nyguo**   _____

4. the land where you live   **noctuyr**   _____

5. put your finger on   **cuhto**   _____

6. as much as you need   **hguone**   _____

Sound of *ou* in *touch*

Super Snoop

Help Tom find his missing dog.
- Mark the path of words that have the same vowel sound as **touch**.
- Read the words.

loud
found
trouble
mound
round
rough
should
couple
young
tough
proud
country
cloud
ground
double
house
out
hound
cousin

The letters **ou** can spell the vowel sound you hear in **touch**. Try that sound to see if it makes a real word.

Sound of *ou* in *touch*

What Is Missing?

A bottle floated onto the beach. Sue looked inside and found a tattered note. Help her read about what happened.

- Write **ew** or **ue** to finish the words.
  Use the word list for help.

brew   blue
due   new
glue   clue
crew   blew

The sky was bl___ ___ that morning when our n___ ___ fishing boat set sail. We had no cl___ ___ as to what was about to happen.

The boat was d___ ___ back at port before sunset. Suddenly a storm started to br___ ___. The wind bl___ ___ so hard that some cr___ ___ members almost fell overboard.

We drifted to shore and looked at our boat. We would need more than gl___ ___ to fix it!

46 Sound of *ew* and *ue* in *new* and *blue*

It's a Mystery

- Use these clues to solve each mystery.

flew blue crew
glue stew due
new
drew

What did the birds do? _____

Why is Tim's bike so shiny? _____

What did Mom make for dinner? _____

What did Dad use to fix the crack? _____

Where did Stan get that picture of a race car? _____

What color is the sky? _____

When do you return a library book? _____

What do you call the sailors on a ship? _____

Sound of *ew* and *ue* in *new* and *blue*

Dinner Call

It's time for dinner.

- Take turns with a partner. Roll a die and move that number of spaces.
- Read aloud the sentence in the box you land on.

We wander home.

Let's stop for water.

We can walk fast.

Red leaves fall from the tall trees.

We watch a small bird on a branch.

You can use magazine cutouts of kids for markers.

48 Sound of *a* and *al* in *water* and *walk*

Juan dropped the ball.

Juan sees his father at the grill.

Lara talks a lot.

We always look both ways before we cross.

We stop to draw with chalk.

Juan will wash his hands.

We are all almost home!

- Make a list of the words that have the vowel sound you hear in **talk.** Notice the different spellings.

Sound of *a* and *al* as in *water* and *walk*

Mystery Meal

summer   early   bird   girl   her   purple

Dad made a surprise for dinner.
- Read the clues.
- Write the words on the lines.

opposite of **him**   h __ __ e
                       1   12

My sister is one.   g __ __ __
                       7

not late   __ a __ __ r
                         2   9

This can chirp.   b __ i __
                       4   11

opposite of **winter** __ __ m __ e __
                             3   8

a color   p u r __ __ __
                       10 5 6

What did Dad make?

__ __ __ __ __ __ __ __ __   __ __ __
 1 2 3 4 5 6 7 8 9   10 11 12

50   R-Controlled Vowels: er, ir, ur, ear

What Did You Expect?

- Take turns with a partner.
- Read each pair of words aloud.
- Write the thing you like best.

	Me	My Partner
water or **milk**		
purple or **red**		
birds or **squirrels**		
Thursday or **Saturday**		
showers or **baths**		
summer or **winter**		
_____ or _____		

Write some other words with **er, ir, ur,** or **ear.**

R-Controlled Vowels: *er, ir, ur, ear*

Word Hunt

Mom has a surprise for us.

- Read the sentences.
- Circle the extra word in each sentence.

1. We We will go on Saturday.
2. We must try to get will there early.
3. We want to see go every act.
4. There to will be thirteen funny clowns.
5. They will the have on purple shirts.
6. They will circus ride bikes in a circle.

What is the surprise?

- Write the words you circled.

_____   _____   _____
       1   2   3

_____   _____   _____
       4   5   6

R-Controlled Vowels: er, ir, ur, ear

Rhyme Time

- Use the word list to finish each line and make a rhyme. All words should have **ear** as in **clear** or **eer** as in **deer**.

near	cheer
year	appear
hear	dear

Did They Forget?

It's almost my birthday.

The date is quite _____.

Will I have to plan

My own party this _____?

Listen! What is that song?

"Happy Birthday," I _____
As I see Mom and Dad

And my sisters _____.

Grandma says, "Did you think

We'd forget you, my _____?"
Then she hugged me and said,

"Surprise! Let's all _____!"

R-Controlled Vowels: *ear, eer* /ir/

Word Hunt

- Read the words in the list.
- Circle each word as you find it in the puzzle.
- A word can go ➡ or ⬇.

Word List

fear	jeer	hear
deer	beard	cheer
near	clear	dear

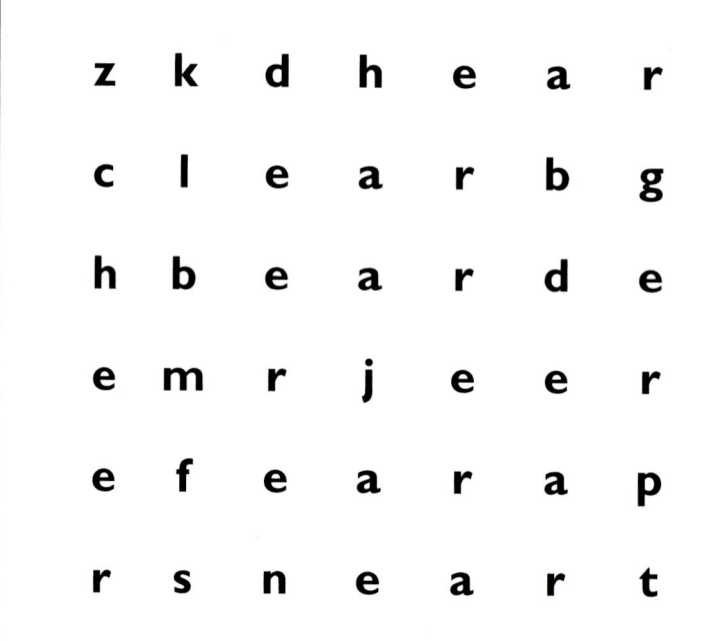

```
z  k  d  h  e  a  r
c  l  e  a  r  b  g
h  b  e  a  r  d  e
e  m  r  j  e  e  r
e  f  e  a  r  a  p
r  s  n  e  a  r  t
```

- Use two of the words to write about a family.

54 R-Controlled Vowels: ear, eer /ir/

On the Road Again

Each word has the **ar** sound as in **park.**

- Write a word for each clue.

1. You see it in the night sky.
   _____

2. This means **not small.**
   _____

3. This means **not soft.**
   _____

4. This is on a tree.
   _____

5. You can ride in this.
   _____

6. This is on a farm.
   _____

- Write a story about a car trip you took.

R-Controlled Vowel: ar 55

Bear Tracks

Big Bear wants to go to the cave.
- Take turns with a partner to write each list word in the game.
- You will need a die and two game markers. Take turns to roll the die.
- Read aloud each word you land on.

Get the bear to the cave first and win!

corn	shore	store	sort
tore	cord	horn	wore
more	fork	form	storm
for	north	porch	fort
torn	worn	born	story

56 R-Controlled Vowels: or, ore

R-Controlled Vowels: or, ore

Horsing Around

Help the horse get to the barn!

- Read all the words aloud.
- Draw a line along the path of words with the sound of **or** as in **more**.

Can you think of any more words with **or**?

Start

corn
rose
purse
shirt
boy
score
forty
tore
horn
her
birth
orange
fern
house
turn
third
coin
fork
near
store
bird
clown
fur

58 R-Controlled Vowels: or, ore

Monkey Business

The monkeys' words are mixed up.
- Read the clues.
- Write the words.

You row a boat with this. ___ ___ ___
                           6   4

number before five ___ ___ ___ ___
                            3

under your feet ___ ___ ___ ___ ___
                 1

to fly high ___ ___ ___ ___
                     5

long, flat piece of wood ___ ___ ___ ___ ___
                                  7

You open this to get inside. ___ ___ ___ ___
                              2   8

Monkey banana words: oolfr, rodo, rsoa, oardb, rao, oufr

*All the words have the same sound that you spell **oar** or **oor** or **our**.*

Why is the jungle so noisy?

There are ___ ___ ___ ___ tigers ___ ___ ___ ___ing.
           1   2   3   4   5   6   7   8

R-Controlled Vowels: oar, oor, our 59

Jungle Code

Miss Shore wrote some directions in code.

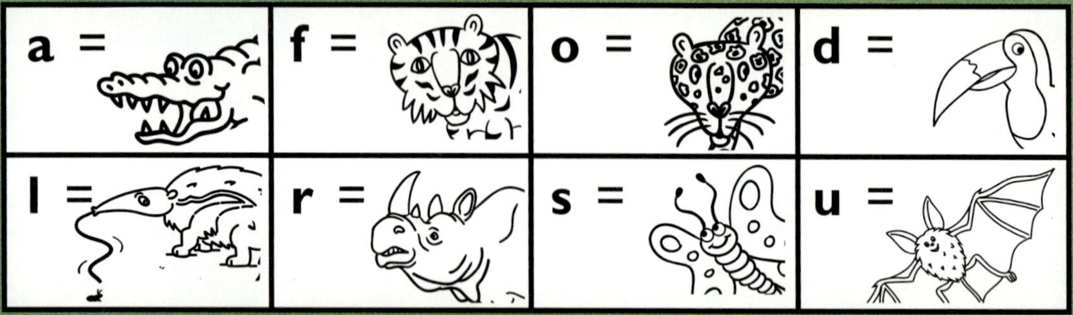

a = (alligator)　f = (tiger)　o = (leopard)　d = (toucan)
l = (anteater)　r = (rhino)　s = (butterfly)　u = (bat)

- Use the code to write the words.

Which things can you do?

1. Please __ __ __ __ like a lion. (rhino, leopard, alligator, rhino) = roar

2. Slide on the __ __ __ __ __ like a snake. (tiger, anteater, leopard, leopard, rhino) = floor

3. Draw __ __ __ __ elephants. (tiger, leopard, bat, rhino) = four

4. Now __ __ __ __ like a bird. (butterfly, leopard, alligator, rhino) = soar

5. Act like a monkey and open the __ __ __ __. (toucan, leopard, leopard, rhino) = door

R-Controlled Vowels: *oar, oor, our*

What Is Missing?

Be fair to your body.
Take care of your health.
Dairy foods make strong bones.
Chicken and rice are a yummy pair.
Fruit is good for you.
Try a pear or an apple.
Eat foods from all 4 groups every day.

Look at this lunch.

- Name the foods you see. Tell which group each comes from.
- Draw one food from the missing group.

This lunch needs a food from the _____ group.

R-Controlled Vowels: *air, are, ear*

A Fair Share

"Pull up a chair," said Blair.
"The pear pie is done."

"Pear pie!" said Gare.
"What a rare treat!"

"Wait a minute, the pair of you!" said Dad.
"I want some, too.
Let's all take a fair share."

Help each person get a fair share of the pie.

- Sort the list words and read them aloud.

bear　stare　tear
hair　wear　share
rare　pair　care
chair　pear　fair

air

are

ear

Fair, share, and **pear** all have the same vowel sound.

R-Controlled Vowels: *air, are, ear*

A Word for It

- Draw lines to match the words with the clues.

1. a lot of water
2. relaxing exercise
3. a yummy food
4. a person who flies an airplane
5. a creature with eight legs
6. not making a sound

yoga
pilot
yogurt
ocean
silent
spider

Are you the pilot of this thing?

- Write about a pilot who has landed in a strange place. Use words from the list.

_____
_____
_____
_____

64 Single Long Vowels

Part II: Medial and Silent Consonants, Consonant Blends, and Digraphs

★ **Parent Pointers**

Skills Medial Consonants • Silent Consonants • Consonant Blends • Consonant Digraphs

Extension Activities

Sound Find
Give your child five letter cards with the letter *t, z, m, r,* or *g* printed on each one. Divide a strip of paper into three sections, representing the beginning, middle, and end of a word. As you say a word, have your child select the letter he or she hears and place the card in the section of the strip of paper that shows whether the letter sound is at the beginning, middle, or end of the word. Use these letters and words: *z- zinnia, lizard, zebra, puzzle; g- wagon, bag, gate, tiger; r- robin, parrot, hammer, carrot; m- melon, camel, drum, lemon; t- kitten, bonnet, table, mitten.*

Skill: Medial Consonants

Blend Quilt
Discuss with your child what a quilt is. Fold and crease a sheet of drawing paper three times. Open the paper to reveal eight sections of a quilt. Draw stitches on the creases and decorate the edges of the quilt. Ask your child to write a word ending with one of the blends *lt, ft, ld,* or *nt* on each section. Then write a sentence or silly rhyme with the word. Circle the consonant blend in each word. Color each section of the quilt.

Skill: Consonant Blend

Give Me a Clue
On a sheet of paper or on an erasable board, write words that contain final consonant digraphs. Make list of words that end in *ch, sh, tch,* and *th*. To play the game, each player gives a clue about one of the words. The player who guesses the answer erases the word and gives a new clue for another word. Play until all words are erased. Use the following examples: *You eat this at noon.* (lunch) *You use this to get clothes white.* (bleach) *This is another word for sofa.* (couch) *You sit on this in the park.* (bench)

Skill: Consonant Digraphs

PARTNER

Website Resources

International Reading Association Parents' Resources
http://www.reading.org

Steck-Vaughn is not responsible for the content of any website listed here. All material is the responsibility of the hosts and creators.

At Home with Phonics 65

Could It Be?

- Find 5 things that **could not** happen. Put an **X** next to each sentence.
- Find 5 things that **could** happen. Put an **O** next to each sentence.

A dragon can ride a bike.

A puppy can sleep.

You can pull a wagon.

What a silly game!

You can play with a puppet.

Medial Consonants

A baby can drive a car.

A rabbit can fly a plane.

A lemon is yellow.

A bunny can drive a truck.

A mitten can be blue.

A goat can spend money.

Medial Consonants

What Is Missing?

Oops! A baby sister spilled milk on this letter. Write the missing letters **dge**, **kn**, or **wr** to read.

Dear Aunt Bridget,

I'm taking care of little Pudge while Dad is on the phone. I was trying to **wr**ite a story, too. I wondered if it should be about a **wr**ecked ship. I decided to write about a drawbri**dge**.

Suddenly, I **kn**ew something was wrong. I looked up. Pudge was **kn**eeling on the e**dge** of the table! She didn't **kn**ow she was in danger. I helped her down. But now there are big smu**dge**s of fu**dge** on my story! Pudge's hands were sticky up to her **wr**ists.

Now I've cleaned Pudge up. I hope she doesn't make more trouble.

Silent Consonants: *dge*, *kn*, *wr*

Riddle Diddles

1 Mom makes a yummy treat. It starts with **f** and rhymes with **budge.**

What is it?_____

2 This is a part of little brother's leg. It can bend. It starts with the letters **kn.**

What is it?_____

3 This is part of little brother's arm. It can bend, too. It starts with the letters **wr.**

What is it?_____

4 Mom uses this to cut up vegetables. It starts with the letters **kn.**

What is it?_____

5 Mom is teaching me to cook. I hope to win one of these. It begins with **b** and ends with **dge.**

What is it?_____

Silent Consonants: _dge_, _kn_, _wr_

Our Aunt Madge

Our Aunt Madge sure knows how to knit.
And she likes it more than just a little bit.

Winter and summer, Aunt Madge keeps on knitting.
You'd think she'd get tired of just sitting and sitting.

Leg warmers, wrist warmers, mittens, and gloves,
She makes them for all of the people she loves.

Some are just right and some are just wrong.
Some are too short and some are too long.

But you be the judge—take a look and you'll see.
It's not the knitting that counts—we know you'll agree.

- Read the poem. The first time you read it, say both the **k** and the **n** in words with **kn**, the **d** and the **g** in words with **dge**, and the **w** and the **r** in words with **wr**. Read the poem again. Say these words correctly.

Silent Consonants: dge, kn, wr

What Pet Is It?

- Read the word in each shape.
- Use green to color the shapes with words that have an **r** sound.

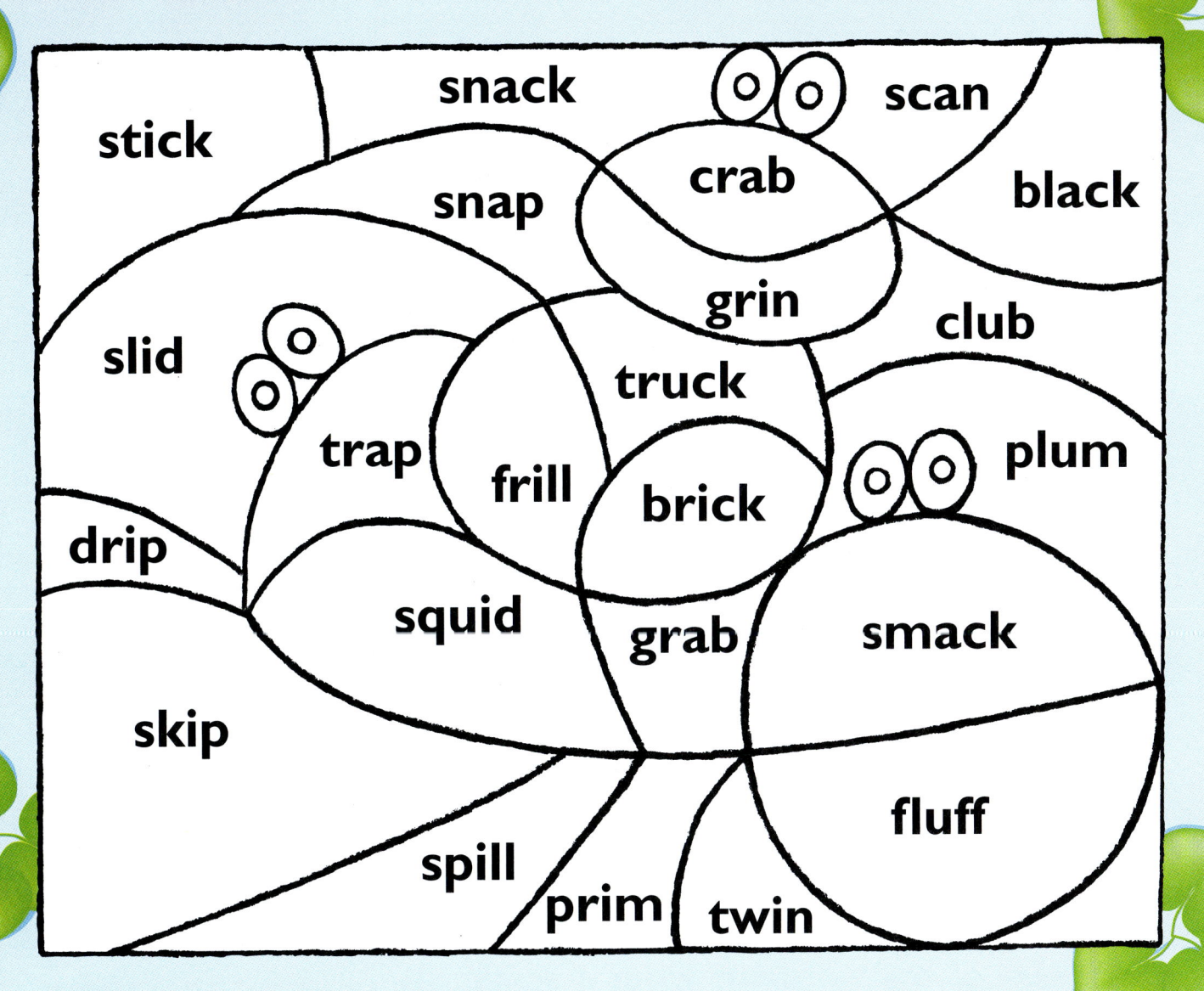

stick, snack, scan, crab, snap, black, slid, grin, club, trap, truck, frill, brick, plum, drip, squid, grab, smack, skip, fluff, spill, prim, twin

- Finish each word that begins with the letters.

bl_____   fl_____   sk_____

sn_____   sp_____   tw_____

cl_____   pl_____   sm_____

Initial 2-Letter Consonant Blends 71

Track the Snake

Help! Stan has lost his pet. It slid away on words that begin with the sounds of **s** and another letter.

- Read each word aloud.
- Draw a line to show where the pet slid.

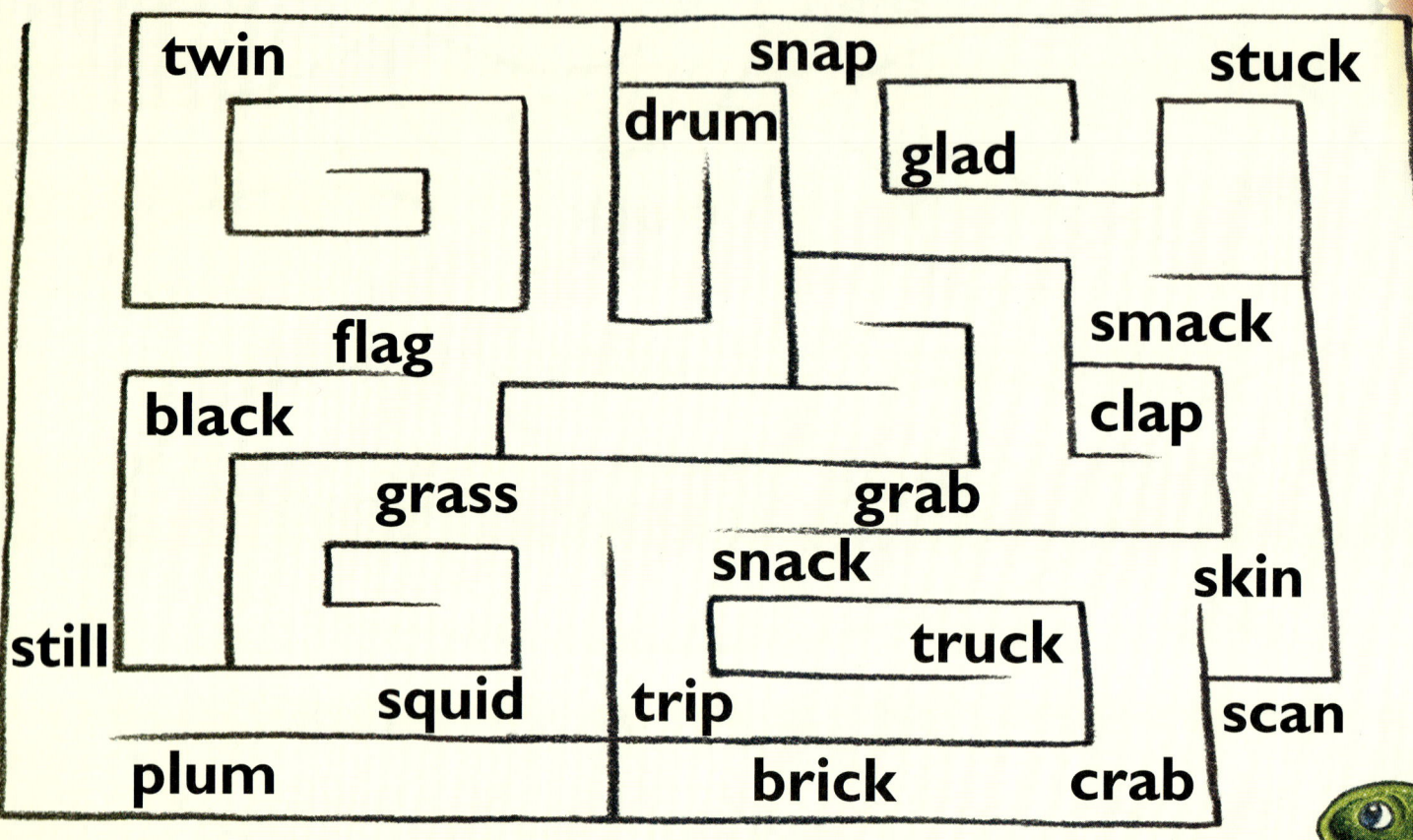

twin   snap   stuck
        drum   glad
                smack
flag   clap
black
    grass   grab
            snack   skin
still   truck
    squid   trip   scan
    plum   brick   crab

- Use two of the words to write a sentence.

_____

_____

_____

72 Initial 2-Letter Consonant Blends

Hill Spill

This very frisky Jack and thirsty Jill
Ran quickly into their house on the hill.
A cup of fresh water made Jill feel glad.
But that rascal Jack jumped up
And of course spilled Jill's cup,
So Jill ran crying to tell her dad.

- Put a line under the words in the rhyme with **cr, fr, gl,** and **sp.**
- Use one of the words in a new rhyme.

Initial 2-Letter Consonant Blends

Hidden Words

• Find and circle the hidden words.

Hidden words in picture: strap, split, shrub, thrill, spring, scrub

• Write and read the words you found.

_____   _____   _____

_____   _____   _____

• Write a sentence. Use a word you found.

_____

_____

74 Initial 3-Letter Consonant Blends

I Spy

- Take turns with a partner to give a clue for a word in the cage.
- Point to the word and say it to answer.

| scrap | thrill | shrub | spring | scrub | struck |
| strip | split | strap | three | shrug | splat |

Now write a clue for one of the words. Have your partner write the answer.

I spy a word that means _____.

_____.

The word is _____.

Initial 3-Letter Consonant Blends

Getting in Shape

- Write the word that fits each shape.
- Write a word that rhymes under each shape.

Look carefully at the shape of each letter.

Word Bank

gold　lift
quilt　mint
craft　bent

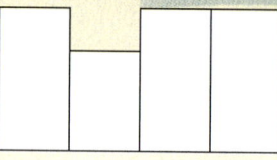

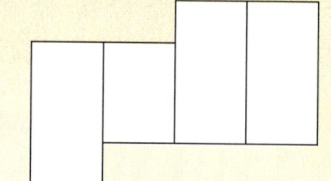

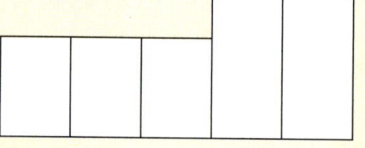

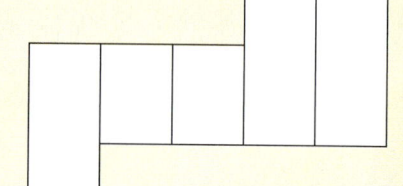

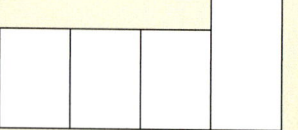

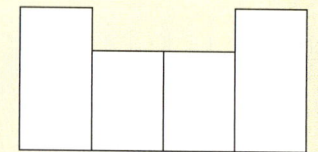

1.
2.
3.
4.
5.
6.

76　Final Consonant Blends *ft, ld, lt, nt*

Fun and Games

- Look at the picture.
- Then follow the directions.

1. Find the cake. Color it yellow.
2. Put an **X** on the mom's hand.
3. Write your name on the cast.
4. Color the vest red.
5. Make an **X** on the mask.
6. Circle the lamp.

Final Consonant Blends *mp, nd, sk, st*

Puzzle Page

- Read each sentence.
- Write the missing word in the puzzle.

Word List

find   spend
stamp wind
send   fast

Across

2. Did you ____ the toy to him?
3. Put the ____ on the mail.
5. I cannot ____ my doll.

Down

1. My toy truck can go ____.
2. Did you ____ nine cents?
4. The ____ made the trees bend.

Remember, there are two ways to say _ind.

78 Final Consonant Blends *mp, nd, sk, st*

Puzzle Page

- Read the clues.
- Write the words.

1. wet − et + hen = _____
2. ship − p + ne = _____
3. the − e + in = _____
4. chin − n + ck = _____
5. is + hop − i = _____
6. whip − ip + eel = _____

- Make up a puzzle for someone to solve.
- Start with one of these words: **whine, thing, show,** or **champ.**

_____

_____

Initial Consonant Digraphs ch, sh, th, wh

Word Hunt

- Circle the words hidden in the picture.
- Then write them on the lines.

Hidden words in picture: this, chain, ship, thick, sheet, whale, wheel, chin

Remember that **th** has two different sounds.

ch

_____
_____

th

_____
_____

wh

_____
_____

sh

_____
_____

Initial Consonant Digraphs ch, sh, th, wh

Wishes

It's fun to think with friends like you
What might happen if our wishes came true.

What would we each make a wish for?
Let's think and talk a little more.

Johnnie would wish to meet a great king.
Beth would wish for a shiny, red ring.

Keith would wish for sacks full of gold.
And I would wish to never get old.

But we need to watch the wishes we make
So we don't receive a surprise that's hard to take!

- Write on paper about a person you wish to meet. Use words that end with **ch**, **sh**, **tch**, or **th**.

Final Consonant Digraphs *ch, sh, tch, th*

Spin on a Star

____sh

____ch ____th

Free ____tch

- Take turns with a partner to spin the spinner.
- Write a word on a little star that ends with the sound you land on. If you land on **Free,** you can fill in any word.
- Write your name by the star. Get the most stars to win!

Final Consonant Digraphs ch, sh, tch, th

____sh

____tch

____sh

____th

____th

____sh

____tch

____ch

Remember **tch** is often used after a **short a, e, i, o,** or **u** sound instead of **ch.**

____sh

____ch

____th

____th

Final Consonant Digraphs *ch, sh, tch, th* 83

Puzzle Page

- Hide the clues with your hand.
- Then read them one line at a time.

Can you solve each puzzle before the last clue?

1
You can eat this.
It may be sweet.
It has a pit.
It rhymes with **reach**.
What is it?
_____

2
It can hide a hole.
It can be in a quilt.
It can be made of cloth.
It ends like **match**.
What is it?
_____

3
It is a hope.
It is a dream.
You may get it.
It rhymes with **dish**.
What is it? _____

4
It may be hot.
It gets you clean.
It gets you wet.
It rhymes with **math**.
What is it? _____

84 Final Consonant Digraphs ch, sh, tch, th

Wish Me Luck

- Read each clue.
- Find the word in the puzzle that answers the clue, and color it green.
- Color the other spaces yellow.

Puzzle words: hang, stick, blank, drank, sting, clock, lock, bank, blink, wing, ring, tank, sick, Jack, kick, pink, sing, dock, honk, wink, sank, thank

Clues

1. You keep money in it.
2. A plane needs it to fly.
3. It means **ill**.
4. It is a name.
5. You can do this to a ball.
6. This is a color.
7. A bee can do this.
8. It may need a key.

Final Consonant Digraphs *ck*, *ng*, *nk*

Word Magic

___ing

___ack

___ank

br

s

___ick

th

cr

___unk

tr

Use letters from the lamp to write words.

86 Final Consonant Digraphs *ck, ng, nk*

Tough Enough

Be a detective.

- Look at the pictures. Find at least four ways that they are different.
- Write about them. Use these words.

laughing

phone

photo

rough

graph

Consonant Digraphs *gh*, *ph* /f/ 87

Double Trouble

Cousin Phil and I used to cause trouble.
You see, he was physically almost my double.
It was tough to see just who was who—
Everyone needed a much bigger clue.

Just when people were about to give up,
Phil would start laughing, and I'd hiccup.
That was it! Now others had their great clue.
They could tell us apart, and you can too.

These words from the poem are in code.

- Figure out the two letters from each picture's word that are needed.
- Write the poem words and read them.

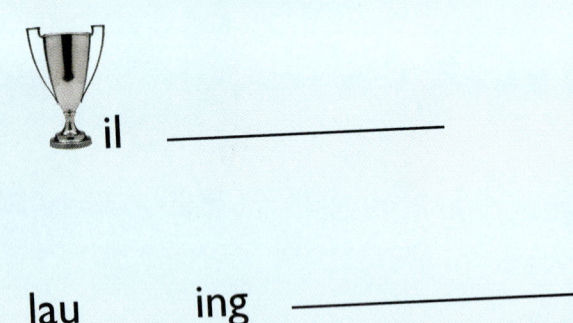

[trophy]il _____

lau [trophy]ing _____

[trophy]ysically _____

tou [mouth laughing] _____

Consonant Digraphs *gh*, *ph* /f/

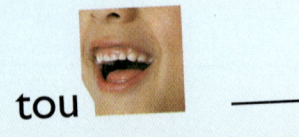

Part III: Verb Endings, Plural Endings, and Comparative Endings

★ **Parent Pointers**

Skills Verb (Action Word) Endings • Plural Endings • Comparative Endings

Extension Activities

Yesterday and Today — **Skill:** Verb Endings

Fold a sheet of paper into three columns. Label one column *Action Word*, label column two *Yesterday*, and label the third column *Today*. Write a list of action words in the first column. Ask your child to write the word with the appropriate endings in the *Yesterday* and *Today* columns. For example, using the action word *paint*, the word *painted* belongs in the *Yesterday* column, and the word *paints* belongs in the *Today* column. Ask your child to write a sentences for each word.

Fold-Overs — **Skill:** Plural Endings

Show your child how to make three fold-overs for words that add *s*, *es*, or change the *y* to *i* and add *es*. Hold each sheet of heavy paper horizontally, and fold the right–hand third of the paper towards the center. Open one of the fold-overs and write *Add s* across the top. Write the singular form of a list of words, such as *jet, cat, ball, clock, pumpkin, pencil, truck*. Fold the flap over and add an *s* ending to each of the words. Write *Add–es* across the top of the second fold-over. Write a list of words that end in *x, s, ss, sh,* or *ch* to which *es* is added to form the plural, such as *box, bus, dress, dish, bench, glass, lunch*. Fold the flap over and add *es* to each of the words to show the plural form. Write *Change y to i and add es* at the top of the third fold-over. Create a fold-over for words that end in y, such as *story, baby, city, penny, pony, family, lady, daisy*. Save the fold-overs to practice reading the words. **Variation:** Fold-overs can be used to practice prefixes and suffixes.

Ed vs. Ing — **Skill:** Verb Endings

Write these words on cards: *move, paste, wipe, love, bake, tape, name, care, hope, race, like, wave, wade, race, bike, skate, share, carve, judge, taste, use, place, make, freeze, drive, bite, smile, save, pile, rake*. Place the cards in a bag. Player one will be Ed and will add *–ed* to each word chosen. Player two will be Ing and will add *–ing* to each word chosen. Players take turns drawing a card from the bag and writing the word with their assigned ending. Did the player remember to drop the final *e* before adding their ending? The player with the most correctly spelled words wins. Add new words and play again.

Website Resources

edhelper.com
http://edhelper.com

aol@school
http://school.aol.com

Steck-Vaughn is not responsible for the content of any website listed here. All material is the responsibility of the hosts and creators.

Joan's Boat

What Joan always wanted the very most
Was to sail a boat along the coast.
One day she strolled by an old, beached boat.
Joan cried, "That's my dream if only it will float!"
For days, she patched and painted coats of blue.
She fixed sails and packed when she was all through.
But then sailing at noon, Joan started to roast.
Soon her poor nose turned as brown as burned toast.
And so she headed her little boat for the shore.
Joan learned sailing alone can be a big chore.

- Name the things Joan did to fix the boat.
- Write about something you have fixed.

What Is Missing?

- Read the sentences.
- Draw what is missing.

A plane landed by the lake.
One little boat sailed on the water.
A big boat floated there, too.
A boy rushed down the road on his bike.

Action Word Ending *ed* 91

Puzzle Page

- Read each sentence.
- Write the missing word in the puzzle.

Across

2. We ____ you on the road yesterday.
4. Mom ____ my lunch.
5. The ship ____ away.

Down

1. Tom ____ me to go with him.
2. We ____ a game.
3. Grace was late and ____ the bus.

Action Word Ending *ed*

Puzzle Page

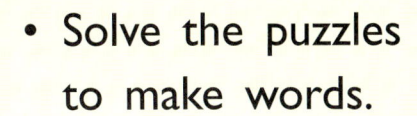

- Solve the puzzles to make words.

    1. skate – e + ing = __ __ __ __ __ __
    2. name – e + ed = __ __ __ __ __
    3. like – e + ing = __ __ __ __ __
    4. close – e + ing = __ __ __ __ __ __
    5. sneeze – e + ed = __ __ __ __ __ __ __
    6. score – e + ed = __ __ __ __ __ __

- Use the letters in the circles to answer.
  What did the cat do when it saw the mouse?

    It __ __ __ __ __ __.
       1 2 3 4 5 6

Action Word Endings *ed, ing* 93

Sheep Shape

- Read the words aloud.
- Take turns adding **ed** and **ing** to make new words.

Remember to drop the **e** before adding **ed** or **ing**.

hike   bake   wipe   use
hope   save

Add **ed**   Add **ing**

_____   _____
_____   _____
_____   _____
_____   _____
_____   _____
_____   _____

94 Action Word Endings *ed, ing*

A Horse Named Glory

Look! Mr. Short is writing a story
About his horse, which he named Glory.

One day, Glory tore across fields, really racing.
Mr. Short was then scared by what he was facing.

Just when the worn out man cried, "No more!"
Glory bucked him off on the squishy, wet shore.

Mr. Short went gliding, z-z-ip, through the air.
He sat in the water, just glaring, o-o-oh, at the mare.

And that's the end of Mr. Short's story
About his horse, which he named Glory.

- Read the poem.
- Read it again. Clap your hands each time you read an action word in which an **e** was dropped before **ed** or **ing** was added.

Action Word Endings *ed, ing* 95

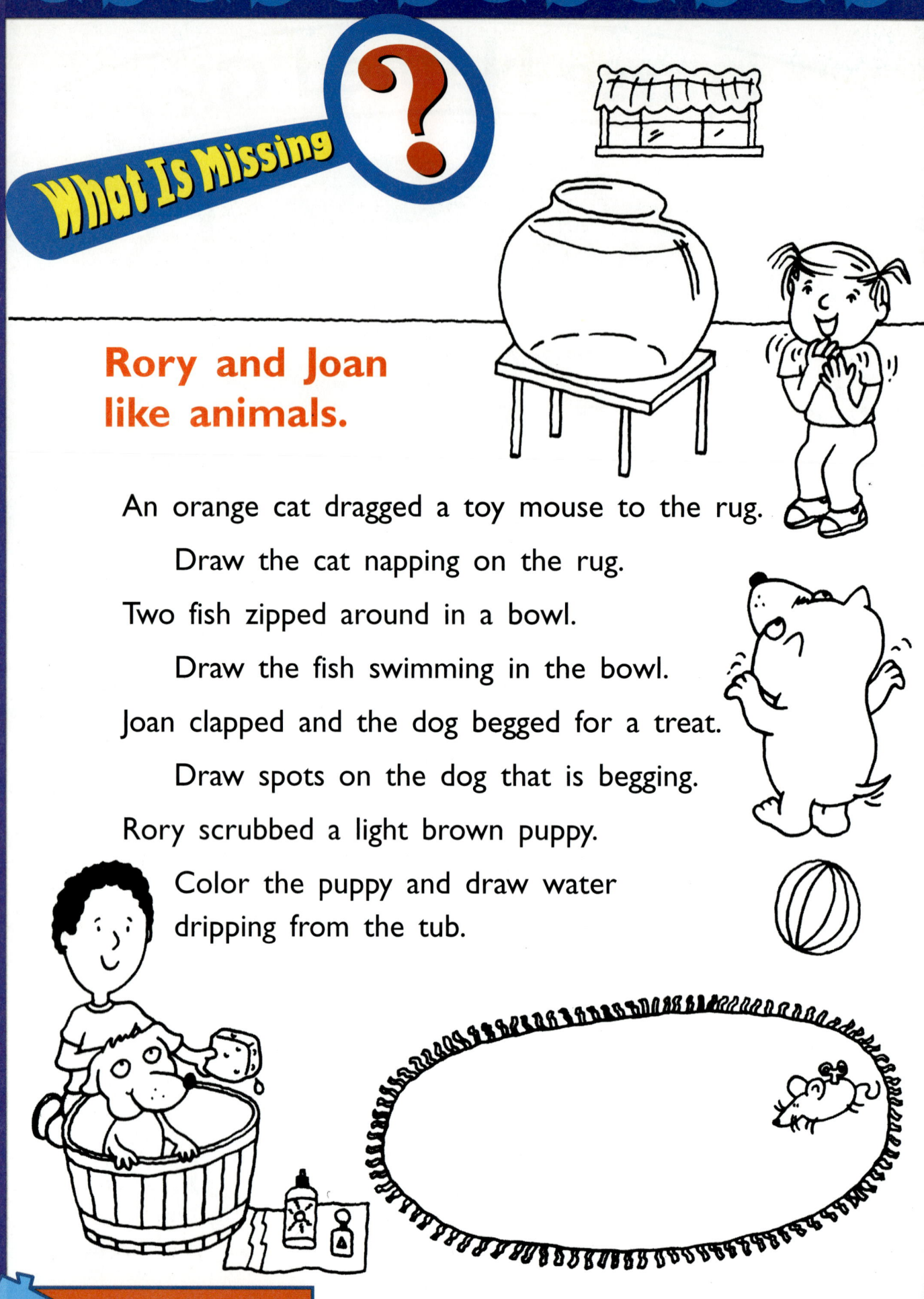

What Is Missing?

Rory and Joan like animals.

An orange cat dragged a toy mouse to the rug.

> Draw the cat napping on the rug.

Two fish zipped around in a bowl.

> Draw the fish swimming in the bowl.

Joan clapped and the dog begged for a treat.

> Draw spots on the dog that is begging.

Rory scrubbed a light brown puppy.

> Color the puppy and draw water dripping from the tub.

96 Action Word Endings *ed, ing*

Word Hunt

What did someone see in a rain forest?

- Cross out the letters **q, x,** and **z.**

```
a x s w i m m i n g z
h i p p o p o p p e d
i t s x h e a d q u p
t w o z c h i m p s z
c h a t t e d z i n q
a z t r e e q z w e x
s a w x a q z w i l d
p i g x r u n n i n g
w e q f l i p p e d a
r o c k z o v e r q z
t o q s e e w o r m s
d i g g i n g q x z q
```

- Now write the sentences you found.

> Remember to use a capital letter at the beginning of a sentence.

Action Word Endings *ed, ing* 97

Put It in Writing!

Rose gets a letter with news from a friend.

- Write what the letter might say.
- Use some action words from the Word List.

Word List

wishes

plays

thanks

watches

helping

thinks

reading

going

waiting

Action Word Endings *es*, *ing*, *s*

What Is Missing?

- Read about the TV show.
- Go to the next page.

TV

Do not miss **Family Fun!**

This week:
- A man watches TV.
- A boy brushes his dog.
- A girl plays with a cat.

Also:
- A girl is jumping rope.
- A boy is kicking a ball.

But soon they are hearing some news that is a surprise!

I am going to watch that show!

Action Word Endings *es, ing, s* 99

On the Trail

A detective hurries around town. She tries to find the suspect. She is worried that it might be too late!

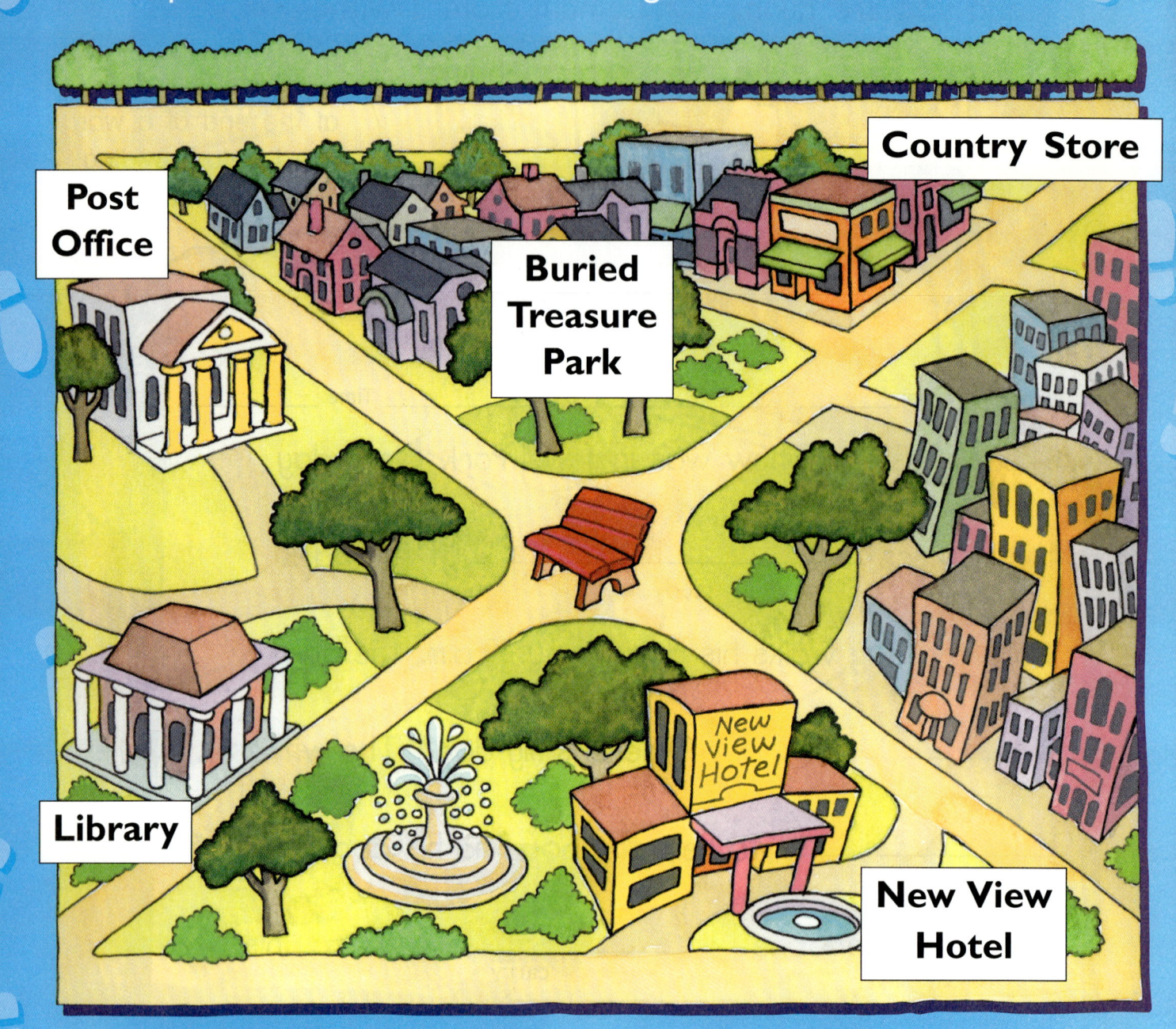

Country Store

Post Office

Buried Treasure Park

Library

New View Hotel

See if the detective and the suspect crossed paths.

- Mark two trails. Use one color for the detective. Use another color for the suspect.

Action Word Endings *ed, ing, es*

Follow the trail of the detective.

- She left the hotel and tried the library, but it was not open yet.
- She went back to the hotel and studied photos.
- She walked to the park bench. She spent ten minutes replying to a letter from her boss.
- She carried her reply to the post office.

Trace the path of the suspect.

- He was spying on shoppers at the store.
- He tried to see if his picture was posted at the post office.
- He sat on the park bench and copied a secret code.
- He carried books back to the library.

What do you think happened next?

_____

_____

_____

Action Word Endings *ed, ing, es*

Puzzle Page

Give me a clue! Give me a clue! Oh, here are a few.

Beth, Will, and Jamal are looking for clues.
One hurries around with a secret codebreaker.
One is carrying a glass that magnifies things.
One has a notebook and a pencil for copying facts.

- **Draw a line to match what each one has.**

Will said, "I copied everything the witness said."
Jamal said, "I relied on the pattern of letters to read the message."
Beth said, "I am studying the fingerprints. We may have a match."

Will

Beth

Jamal

104 Action Word Endings *ed, ing, es*

Jeanette the Sleepyhead

Jeanette is such a sleepyhead,
Her mom can't get her out of bed.
Mom calls out, "It's time to be on your way.
You can't sleep like a bear in winter all day.
New babies don't snooze as much as you do.
Someday we'll tell stories about sleepy you."
When Mom finally says, "You'll have to walk fast,"
Jeanette jumps up and gets ready at last.

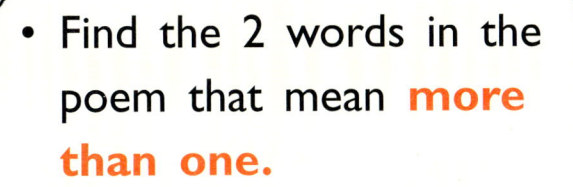

- Find the 2 words in the poem that mean **more than one.**
- Write to change the words so they mean **only one.**

More Than One   **Only One**

_____   _____

_____   _____

Plural Endings s, es   105

Good Timing

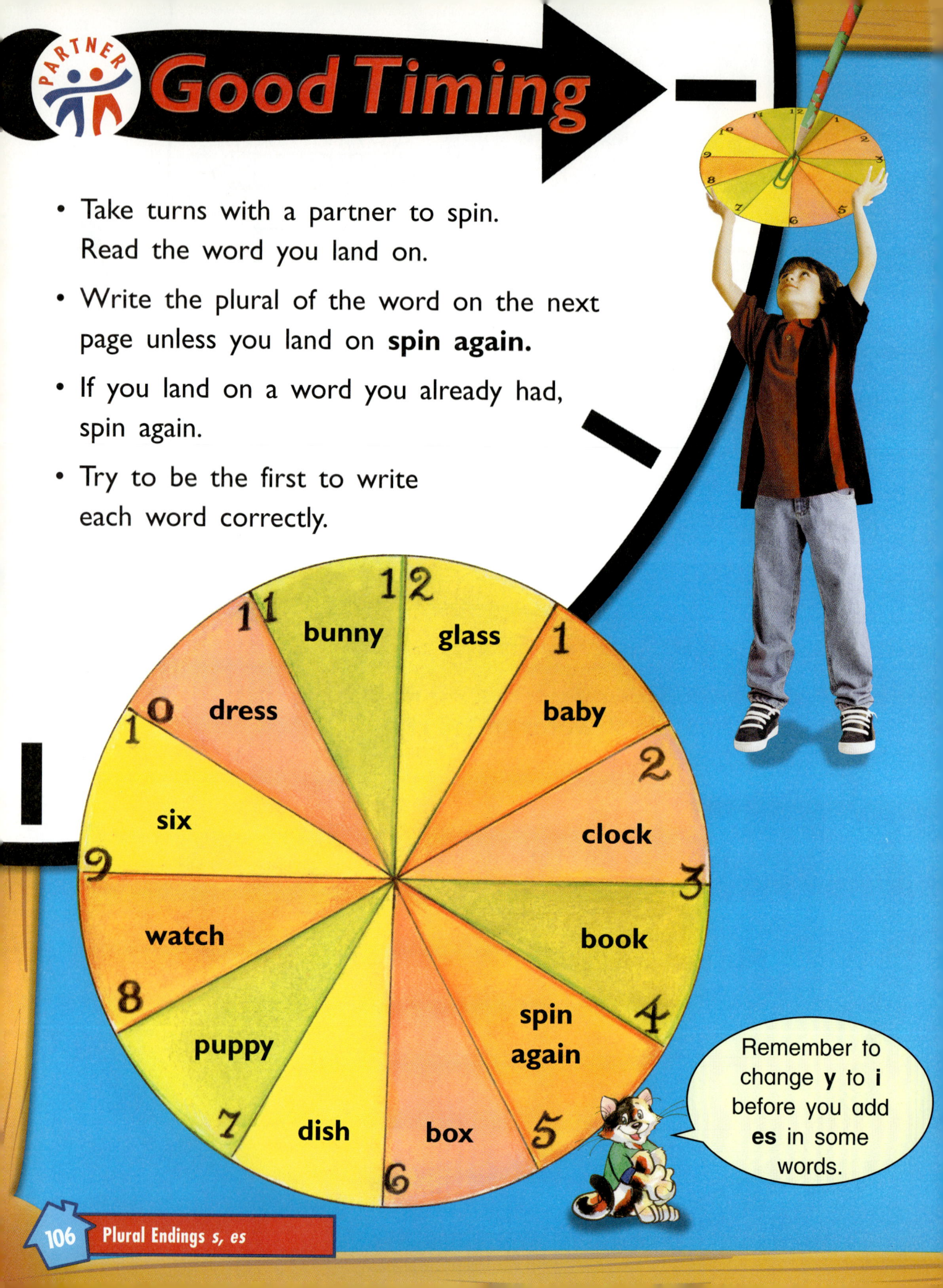

- Take turns with a partner to spin. Read the word you land on.
- Write the plural of the word on the next page unless you land on **spin again.**
- If you land on a word you already had, spin again.
- Try to be the first to write each word correctly.

Spinner words:
1. glass
2. baby
3. clock
4. book
5. spin again
6. box
7. dish
8. puppy
9. watch
10. six
11. dress
12. bunny

Remember to change **y** to **i** before you add **es** in some words.

106 Plural Endings s, es

Plural Endings *s, es*

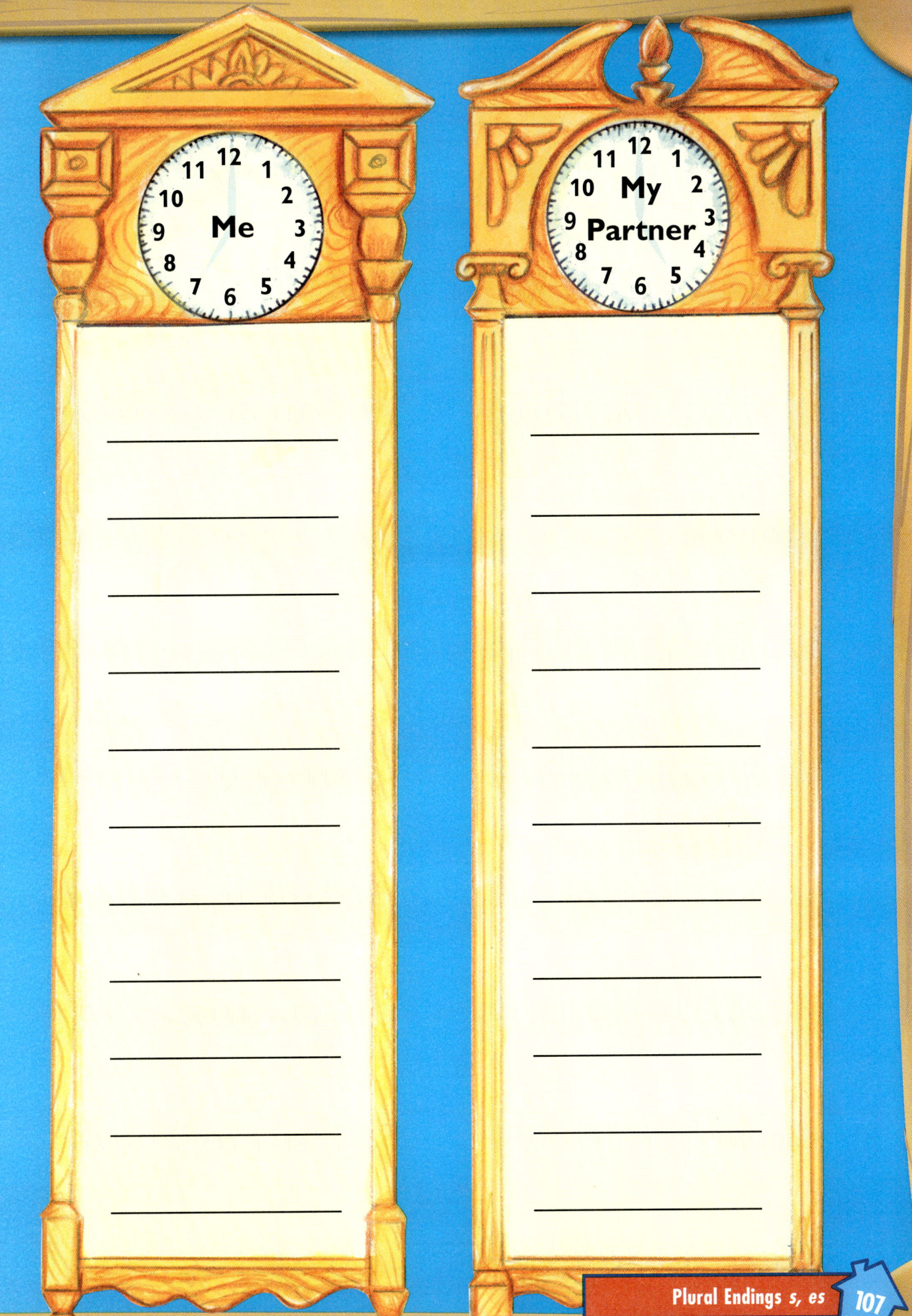

Clock Club

- Crack the Clock Club's code.

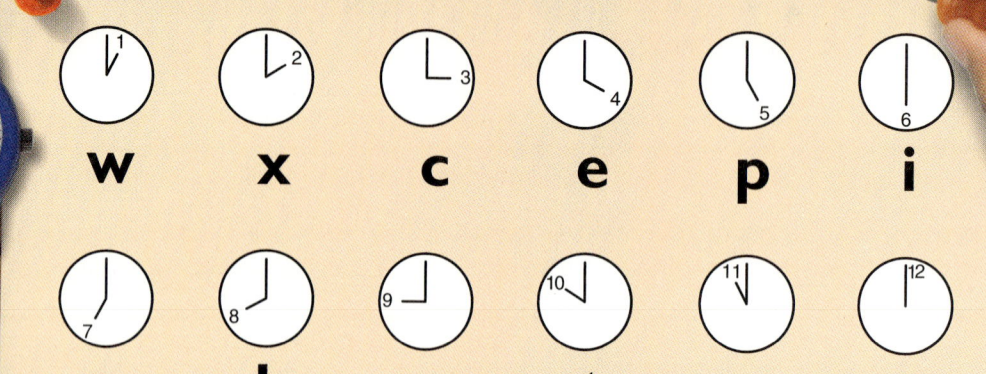

1=w	2=x	3=c	4=e	5=p	6=i
7=a	8=h	9=s	10=t	11=n	12=g

Come to Clock Club this week.

Dues are ten __p__ __e__ __n__ __n__ __i__ __e__ __s__.

Bring some clocks or __w__ __a__ __t__ __c__ __h__ __e__ __s__.

You will find out many new __t__ __h__ __i__ __n__ __g__ __s__.

Plural Endings *s, es*

The Tick-Tock Shop

Remember to change the **f** to **v** before adding **es**.

- Read the words on the clocks.
- Change each word to mean more than one.

1. wife
2. elf
3. leaf
4. self
5. shelf
6. loaf
7. scarf
8. life

1 _____   2 _____
3 _____   4 _____
5 _____   6 _____
7 _____   8 _____

Who keep the clocks working? _____

Plural Ending es 109

A Day at a Time

- Read about the busy week.

Sunday	Meet Mr. Feather's **wife**
Monday	Buy a new **scarf**
Tuesday	Get ready to paint other **half** of house
Wednesday	Rake the **leaves**
Thursday	Put up **shelf** in den
Friday	Bake three **loaves** of bread
Saturday	See **wolves** at the zoo

- Make a chart on paper.
- Write the **red** words.
- Change each word to mean **one** or **more than one**.

One	More Than One
wife	wives

Plural Ending *es*

The Fairest Tree

I have the fairest tree.
Nothing did it bear
But the tiniest of apples
And a still littler pear.

The apple was bright and fatter.
The pear was curvier to see.
I washed both for Clare to eat
Since she was hungrier than me.

So now my fairest tree
Is looking a little bare.
I really hope it quickly grows
More for us to share!

- Write the missing words with **er** or **est.**

fair	fairer	_____
tiny	tinier	_____
fat	_____	fattest
curvy	_____	curviest
hungry	_____	hungriest

Comparative Endings *er, est*

The Greatest Picnic

Jane had the greatest day of her life.

- Read the sentences.
- Write to finish the words that have **er** or **est**.

Remember sometimes you add or take away a letter to add an ending.

1. A sunny day is nice_____ than a rainy one for a picnic.

2. It is hot_____ in the sun than it is in the shade.

3. Apple juice is sweet_____ than lemonade.

4. These are the thin_____ chips I have ever eaten.

5. Foot-long hot dogs are the long_____ kind.

6. Hot dogs grill fast_____ than chicken.

7. This watermelon is big_____ than a football.

8. It is the ripe_____ one I have ever tasted.

Comparative Endings er, est

Part IV: Suffixes, Prefixes, Contractions, Compound Words, and Possessives

★ **Parent Pointers**

Skills Suffixes • Prefixes • Contractions • Compound Words
• Singular and Plural Possessives

Extension Activities

Silly Verses — **Skill:** Suffixes

Stimulate your child's interest by singing the song, "Row, Row, Row Your Boat." Create new verses to this familiar song by changing the words *gently* and *merrily* to other words ending with *ly*. For example:

Row, row, row your boat, *briskly* down the stream.

Quickly, quickly, quickly, quickly, life is but a dream.

Happiness is… — **Skill:** Suffixes

The suffix *ness* means "a state of" when added to a word. The word *happiness* means a "state of being happy." Write the words *Happiness is …* on a sheet of paper or on an erasable board and list all the things that create a "state of being happy" for your child. A variation of this activity is to have your child do a *Kindness is …*

Word Chain — **Skill:** Compound Words

Write a compound word at the top of a sheet of paper or on an erasable board. Challenge your child to use the last word of the compound word to begin a new compound word. Write the word under the first word and begin a list. Create a chain of words such as *sailboat, boathouse, housetop, topcoat*. Your child can write each word on a strip of paper and create a paper chain of compound words.

PARTNER

Website Resources

Rigby Education resources for Parents, Kids, and Teachers
www.rigby.com

Steck-Vaughn is not responsible for the content of any website listed here. All material is the responsibility of the hosts and creators.

At Home with Phonics 113

My Neighbor's Sleigh

My neighbor has a huge red sleigh.
Eight hundred pounds is what it must weigh.
He's careful how he parks it in the spring,
His yard is so very tiny for that big thing.
On sunny summer days, the sleigh sits in the heat,
Looking shiny and still with its row of bells neat.
But when the weather turns cold and snow begins to fall,
It's a wonderful, joyful treat for us all!

- Circle the words with the suffix **ful** or **y** at the end.
- Use these words to write your own poem.

_____
_____
_____
_____
_____

Put It in Writing!

You can use words with **ful** or **y** at the end to tell what things are like.

It was a stormy spring day. Lightning flashed in the sky. The weather was too windy and rainy for us to play outside. We were careful as we made our way up to the attic.

What happens next?

- Use words like **scary, shiny, slimy, dusty, fuzzy, helpful, graceful, playful,** and **thankful.**

Suffixes *ful, y*

What Do You Think?

1. Does the sun rise **daily, weekly, monthly,** or **yearly?**
   _____

2. Do you greet winter **happily** or **sadly?**
   _____

3. Does the wind blow **softly** or **briskly** in spring?
   _____

4. Does summer go by **quickly** or **slowly?**
   _____

5. Do snowflakes brush your cheek **gently** or sting it **sharply?**
   _____

Suffix ly

Word Hunt

- Read the words in the list.
  Find and circle each word in the puzzle. A word can be → or ↓.

You can hunt for words in any season.

Word List

sadly   fairly
coldly quietly
happily clearly
loudly softly
dimly   warmly
monthly speedily

```
x c l e a r l y
h a p p i l y x
q m o n t h l y
s p e e d i l y
s a d l y e o t
o d i m l y u m
f a i r l y d r
t e w a r m l y
l c o l d l y w
y q u i e t l y
```

Suffix ly

Fitness for You

Fitness is the state of being fit.

What are you doing about your own fitness? Taking part in a sport is one good way to become more fit. What do players in different sports need?

When you add **ness** to the end of a describing word, you're talking about the state of being like that.

- Unscramble the words to find out.

Runners need **nessckqui**. _____

Football players need **outghness**. _____

Tumblers need **nesssteaid**. _____

No matter what sport you play,

winning brings **ahpipness**, _____

and losing brings some **dassens**. _____

You have to work hard to reach **eatnessgr**. _____

- Name a sport you like. Use words with **ness** to tell what it takes to play that sport.

118 Suffix *ness*

Word Hunt

- Find and circle words from the list. A word can go ⟶ or ↓.

Word List

fit	happy	kind
sharp	loud	sleepy
great	lazy	rainy
sweet	ill	thin

```
g  l  f  i  t  s  x
r  a  i  n  y  w  p
e  z  l  k  s  e  h
a  y  l  i  h  e  a
t  h  i  n  a  t  p
l  o  u  d  r  g  p
s  l  e  e  p  y  y
d  n  l  p  n  l  n
```

- Now add **ness** to each word. Remember that you might need to change **y** to **i**.

_____   _____

_____   _____

_____   _____

_____   _____

_____   _____

_____   _____

Suffix *ness* 119

Puzzle Page

The answers end with **able**. Remember the spelling rules before you add that suffix.

Clues

1. Our softball team would like to forget last year.

   That was a _____ season.

2. This year, though, no one could stop us.

   We were not _____.

3. I can't believe how much better we were.

   It was not _____.

4. We learn things quickly. Coach Jenny says that we are

   _____.

5. We all really admire her. We think she is an

   _____ person.

6. We will remember what we learned from her. Maybe next year no one will beat us. We will not be _____.

Suffix *able*

Suffix *able*

Puzzle Page

All the words in the puzzle begin with **dis** or **un**.

1. We don't have much trash at our house, because my sister always finds a use for _____ paper.

Prefixes *dis, un*

2. When she gets a gift wrapped in paper, she _____ it carefully so she can reuse the paper.

3. Usually I trust my sister, but sometimes I _____ her ideas.

4. I like having nice covers on my books, but I _____ it when she puts fancy paper on them.

5. I like to appear cool, so I want to _____ when I pull out a book covered in bright pink paper.

6. Even if I lock my book bag, my sister always finds a way to _____ it.

Prefixes *dis, un* 123

It's a Different Story!

- Read the story. Then add the word part **dis** or **un** in each blank.

Remember that **dis** and **un** both mean **not** or the **opposite** of something.

Sam was going home. He was very ____happy.

He ____packed his bags, ____tied his shoes,

and ____locked the door. He walked outside.

A rainbow had ____appeared.

Sam ____liked sitting while he waited.

Finally, his parents arrived to take him home. Sam said, "Tom told me this was one of the most beautiful places on Earth. Now I ____believe him."

- Read the story with your changes.
- Draw a picture to show how the story has changed.

Prefixes dis, un

Mix It Up!

- Read and say each word part.
- Put the word cards together to write words.

_____

_____

_____

_____

_____

_____

_____

_____

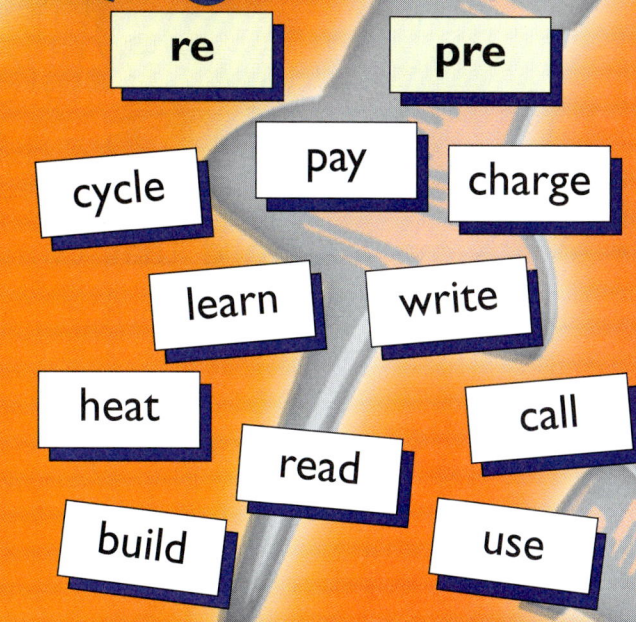

re   pre

cycle   pay   charge

learn   write

heat   call

read

build   use

- Use as many of your words as you can to make a poster about taking care of the Earth.

Remember that **pre** means **before** and **re** means **again.**

Prefixes pre, re 125

Puzzle Page

- Write the list word that completes each sentence in the puzzle.

preview   retell
reuse   preheat
preschool

1. ___ the oven before you put food in it to cook.

2. You can ___ paper bags.

3. Children go to ___ before they go to kindergarten.

4. David likes to ___ stories over and over.

5. Before you buy a book, ___ the pages.

126 Prefixes *pre, re*

Peter Piper Picked a Peck...

If the twister about Peter Piper seems easy to you,
I wish you'd help me know what to do.
Even when I preview the lines in my head,
Something very strange comes out instead.
I restart and retry until I'm almost blue.
My tongue gets lazy, beyond fixing—it's true.
What? You want me to try the one about a woodchuck?
Then please prearrange delivery of lots of luck.

- Try saying the tongue twister "Peter Piper Picked a Peck of Pickled Peppers."
- Then make up your own tongue twister. Use at least one word with **pre** and one word with **re**.

Prefixes pre, re

Contraction Action

- Take turns with a partner to spin the spinner.
- Read the words by that number on your list.
- Write the contraction that means the same.
- If you already had a word, wait for your next turn.
- You win when you fill your word boxes.

Remember that **'d** can mean **would** or **had**.

Player 1
1. I would
2. I have
3. we are
4. she had
5. could have
6. we would

Player 2
1. you are
2. you would
3. we have
4. they are
5. they had
6. should have

128 Contractions with 'd, 're, 've

○ **My Words**

_____

_____

_____

_____

_____

_____

○ **My Partner's Words**

_____

_____

_____

_____

_____

_____

- Switch lists and play again.

Contractions with 'd, 're, 've   129

Paint Pairs

- Read the words to someone.
- Match the words with their contractions.
- Color each matching pair with a different color.

they would · you are

you're · you'd · they've · we have

you have · we're · they'd · you've

we've · we are · they have · you had

Contractions with 'd, 're, 've

Let's Remember

- Make 24 word cards like these.

I will	he will	is not	isn't	he'll
will not	let's	let us	you will	I'll
they'll	she's	won't	I'm	she is
I am	you'll	here's	it's	
here is	has not	hasn't		
it is	they will			

- Mix the cards and put them facedown in rows.

- Take turns with a partner. Turn two cards faceup and read the words aloud.

- If the words go together, keep the cards. If they do not match, turn them facedown again.

- Play until you match all the cards.

You'll have to think really hard!

Contractions with 'll, 'm, n't, 's

Tommy Tootle

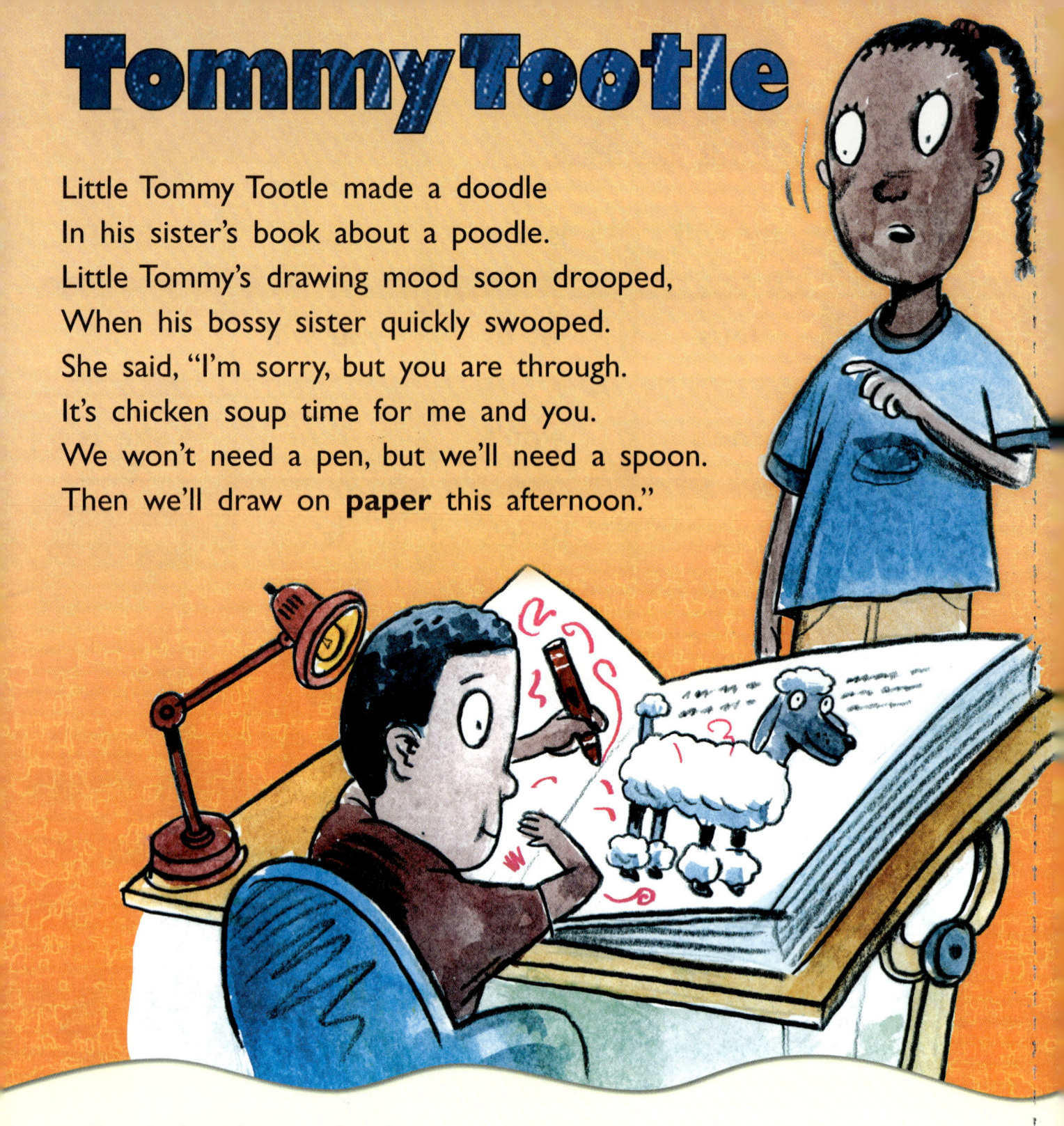

Little Tommy Tootle made a doodle
In his sister's book about a poodle.
Little Tommy's drawing mood soon drooped,
When his bossy sister quickly swooped.
She said, "I'm sorry, but you are through.
It's chicken soup time for me and you.
We won't need a pen, but we'll need a spoon.
Then we'll draw on **paper** this afternoon."

- Read the rhyme aloud.
- Then circle the words with ' that stand for two words.
- Read the rhyme again. Say the two words that each word you circled stands for.

Contractions with 'll, 'm, n't, 's

Word Hunt

- Read the words in the paint.
- Circle the words in the puzzle that mean the same.

Paint palette words: do not, does not, he is, cannot, I am, let us, she will, what is, there is, who will

d	o	e	s	n	'	t	p	m
s	b	c	w	h	o	'	l	l
h	e	t	h	e	r	e	'	s
g	k	d	a	'	d	j	l	l
'	p	o	t	s	m	f	'	o
c	a	n	'	t	n	s	m	q
r	t	'	s	h	e	'	l	l
l	e	t	'	s	u	w	l	v

Contractions with 'll, 'm, n't, 's

Amazing Tricks

Can you change two words into one?

- Look at each pair of pictures.
- Write the compound word. Read the words.

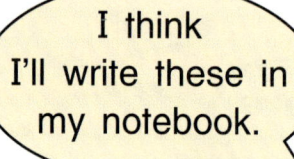

I think I'll write these in my notebook.

toothbrush

134 Compound Words

Puzzle Page

- Use the letters to make words that can go together as compound words.
- The words go down and then across.

cbwy
c
b o y
w

rincot
a

bubah
t

- Write each compound word.

____

____

____

Word Surprise

What on earth is a flowerlight?
It is **flower**pot + **flash**light.

- Read the words in the list.
- Mix up the words to write silly new ones.

cheeseburger	sailboat
bathtub	cowboy
birdbath	paintbrush
butterfly	raincoat

_____ + _____ = _____

_____ + _____ = _____

_____ + _____ = _____

Draw a picture of one of your surprise words.

136 Compound Words

Hidden Surprises

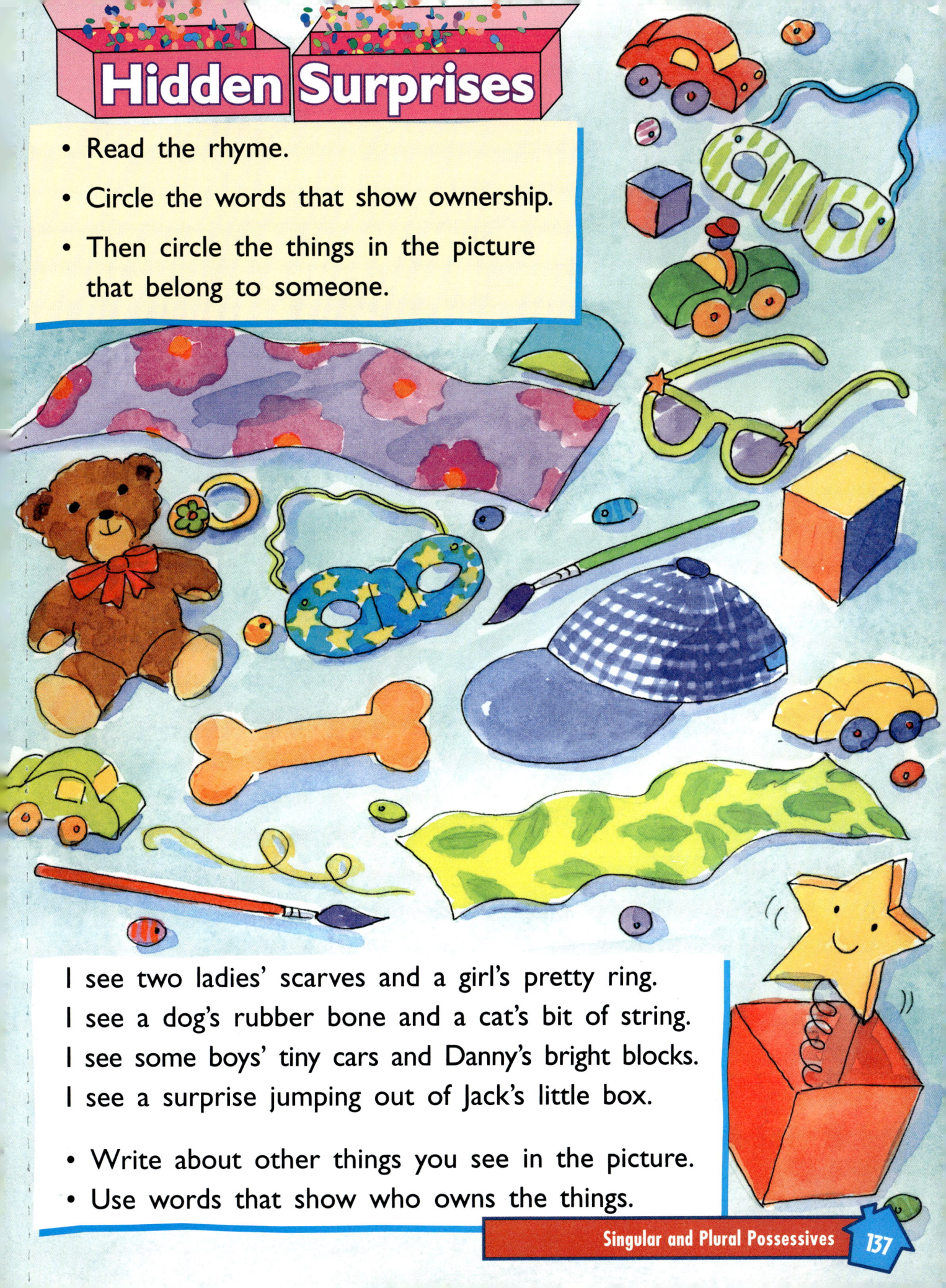

- Read the rhyme.
- Circle the words that show ownership.
- Then circle the things in the picture that belong to someone.

I see two ladies' scarves and a girl's pretty ring.
I see a dog's rubber bone and a cat's bit of string.
I see some boys' tiny cars and Danny's bright blocks.
I see a surprise jumping out of Jack's little box.

- Write about other things you see in the picture.
- Use words that show who owns the things.

Singular and Plural Possessives 137

Look Who's Talking

- Read what each animal said.

"My shirt has stripes."

"My skirt has dots."

"Our hats fell off."

"My coat is big."

"We have long tails."

"We can use ' to show that someone has or owns something."

- Complete each sentence. Use words with **'s** or **s'**.

The _____ _____ has dots.

The _____ _____ fell off.

The _____ _____ is big.

The _____ _____ are long.

The _____ _____ has stripes.

138 Singular and Plural Possessives

Answer Key

Page

8	cat: bat, pack, an; pig: it, pin, hid; bug: mud, tub, fun
9	Jack/sack; pig/wig/big; in/pin; run/fun; map/cap; lip/tip; rub/tub; bug/rug
10	1. cup, 2. pan, 3. hat; cat
11	1. rock 2. top 3. bed 4. mess
13	1. time, 2. fine, 3. broke, 4. tape, 5. tone, 6. bike, 7. fuse, 8. gate; plane
14	a bake set, a red kite, a cute doll, a jump rope, a little bike
15	Color: day, trail, stay, brain, lane, tray, clay, rain, spray, pail, train, say, may, gray
18	1. funny, 2. me, 3. piggy, 4. happy, 5. empty, 6. he, 7. money, 8. valley
19	Follow the path: eat, creep, green, see, meal, bean, queen, jeep, heat
21	The bat and ball are missing. Words include: Neil, field, Sheila, relief
22	seize the thief
23	Cy
24	Color: pie, by, why, cry, die, try, spy, lie, shy. Answer: fly a plane
25	1. bow, 2. blow, 3. throw, 4. snow, 5. crow, 6. low
26	snow, blow, mow, grow
27	1. road, 2. float, 3. toast, 4. soap, 5. croak, 6. soak, 7. boat, 8. toad
28	goat, coat, throat, toast, soap, coast, croak, goal, loaf, oak
29	Message: Did you see a bright light in the sky last night?
30	1. not low, 2. flight, 3. not dark or not heavy, 4. night, 5. not wrong or not left, 6. might
31	1. sleigh, 2. eighteen, 3. weight, 4. neighbor, 5. eight, 6. neigh
32	a sleigh
34	1. hawk, 2. pause, 3. thaw, 4. fawn, 5. paw, 6. haul, 7. taught, 8. straw
35	1. head, 2. bread, 3. heavy, 4. thread, 5. sweat
36	ready, head, ahead, sweat, heavy, breath, steady
37	1. pout, 2. down, 3. count, out, loud 4. frown, 5. sound
38	Bottom: ground, round, brown, wound, Wow, shouted
39	when you are a mouse
42	You should look at me and smile.
44	1. rough, 2. tough, 3. young, 4. country, 5. touch, 6. enough
45	trouble, rough, young, couple, tough, country, double, cousin
46	blue, new, clue, due, brew, blew, crew, glue
47	flew, new, stew, glue, drew, blue, due, crew
50	her, girl, early, bird, summer, purple. Dad made hamburger pie.
52	We will go to the circus.
53	near, year, hear, appear, dear, cheer
55	1. star, 2. large, 3. hard, 4. bark, 5. car, 6. barn
58	corn, score, store, fork, horn, forty, tore, orange
59	oar, four, floor, soar, board, door; There are four tigers roaring.
60	1. roar, 2. floor, 3. four, 4. soar, 5. door
61	This lunch needs a food from the fats group.
63	air: hair, pair, chair, fair; are: stare, share, rare, care; ear: bear, tear, wear, pear
64	1. ocean, 2. yoga, 3. yogurt, 4. pilot, 5. spider, 6. silent
68	write, wrecked, drawbridge, knew, kneeling, edge, know, smudges, fudge, wrists
69	1. fudge, 2. knee, 3. wrist, 4. knife, 5. badge
71	black, fluff, skip, snap or snack, spill, twin, club, plum, smack
72	still, squid, snack, skin, smack, snap, stuck, scan
73	Underline: frisky, fresh, glad, spilled, crying
74	split, spring, shrub, thrill, scrub, strap

At Home with Phonics

Answer Key

Page

76 1. lift, 2. gold, 3. craft, 4. quilt, 5. mint, 6. bent

78 Across- 2. send, 3. stamp, 5. find, Down- 1. fast, 2. spend, 4. wind

79 1. when, 2. shine, 3. thin, 4. chick, 5. shop, 6. wheel

80 ch- chain, chin, wh- whale, wheel, th- this, thick, sh- sheet, ship

84 1. peach, 2. patch, 3. wish, 4. bath

85 1. bank, 2. wing, 3. sick, 4. Jack, 5. kick, 6. pink, 7. sting, 8. lock

86 Possible answers: bring, brick, sing, sack, sick, thing, thank, thick, crack, crank, crick, track, trick, trunk

88 Phil, laughing, physically, tough

92 Across: 2. passed, 4. packed, 5. sailed; Down: 1. asked, 2. played, 3. missed

93 1. skating, 2. named, 3. liking, 4. closing, 5. sneezed, 6. scored; It smiled.

94 Add ed: hiked, hoped, baked, wiped, saved, used; Add ing: hiking, hoping, baking, wiping, saving, using

95 Drop e to add ing: writing, racing, facing, gliding, glaring

97 A swimming hippo popped its head up. Two chimps chatted in a tree. We saw a wild pig running. We flipped a rock over to see worms digging.

101 studies, cried, tried, carrying, copied

104 Will has the notebook. Beth has the magnifying glass. Jamal has the secret codebreaker.

105 babies/baby, stories/story

108 pennies, watches, things

109 1. wives, 2. elves, 3. leaves, 4. selves, 5. shelves, 6. loaves, 7. scarves, 8. lives; The elves keep the clocks working.

110 The changed words are wives, scarves, halves, leaf, shelves, loaf, wolf

111 fairest, tiniest, fatter, curvier, hungrier

112 1. nicer, 2. hotter, 3. sweeter, 4. thinnest, 5. longest, 6. faster, 7. bigger, 8. ripest

114 Circle: careful, sunny, shiny, very, tiny, wonderful, joyful

118 quickness, toughness, steadiness, happiness, sadness, greatness

119 fitness, happiness, kindness, sharpness, loudness, sleepiness, greatness, laziness, raininess, sweetness, illness, thinness

121 forgettable, stoppable, believable, teachable, admirable, beatable

123 1. unused, 2. unwraps, 3. distrust, 4. dislike, 5. disappear, 6. unlock

124 unhappy, unpacked, untied, unlocked, disappeared, disliked, disbelieve

125 Possible answers: reuse, recycle, rebuild, reheat, recall, rewrite, reread, repay, recharge, relearn, preheat, prepay

126 1. preheat, 2. reuse, 3. preschool, 4. retell, 5. preview

129 Player 1: I'd, I've, we're, she'd, could've, we'd; Player 2: you're, you'd, we've, they're, they'd, should've

130 Matching pairs: they would/they'd, you are/you're, we have/we've, you have/you've, we are/we're, they have/they've, you had/you'd

131 Matching cards: I will/ I'll, he will/ he'll, is not/ isn't, will not/ won't, let us/ let's, you will/ you'll, she is/ she's, I am/ I'm, here is/ here's, has not/hasn't, it is/ it's, they will/ they'll

132 I'm/ I am, it's / it is, won't/ will not, we'll/ we will, we'll/ we will

133 Circle: Across: doesn't, who'll, there's, can't, she'll, let's; Down: don't, what's, he's, I'm

134 watchdog, raincoat, birdhouse, starfish, cupcake, mailbox

135 cowboy, raincoat, bathtub

137 Circle the words: ladies', girl's, dog's, cat's, boys', Danny's, Jack's, Circle the objects: scarves, ring, bone, string, cars, blocks, box

138 The pig's skirt has dots. The birds' hats fell off. The cat's coat is big. The dogs' tails are long. The frog's shirt has stripes.

140 Core Skills

Phonics Skills Checklist

Page	Skill	Mastered	Needs Practice
8–10	Short *a*, *i*, and *u*		
11–12	Short *e* and *o*		
13–14	Long vowel: *CVCe*		
15–16	Long a: *ai, ay*		
17–18	Long e: *Ce, y, ey*		
19–20	Long e: *ea, ee*		
21–22	Long e: *ei, ie*		
23–24	Long i: *Cie, Cy, CCy*		
25–26	Long o: *Co, ow*		
27–28	Long o: *oa*		
29–30	Long i: *igh*		
31–32	Long a: *eigh*		
33–34	Sound of *au* and *aw*		
35–36	Sound of *ea* in *head*		
37–39	Sound of *ou* and *ow* in *house/how*		
40–41	Sound of *oi* and *oy*		
42–43	Sound of *oo/ou* in *took/would*		
44–45	Sound of *ou* in *touch*		
46–47	Sound of *ew/eu* in *new/blue*		
48–49	Sound of *a/al* in *water/walk*		
50–52	R-Controlled Vowels: *er, ir, ur, ear*		
53–54	R-Controlled Vowels: *ear, eer, /ir/*		
55	R-Controlled Vowel: *ar*		
56–58	R-Controlled Vowels: *or, ore*		
59–60	R-Controlled Vowels: *oar, oor, our*		
61–63	R-Controlled Vowels: *air, are, ear*		
64	Single Long Vowels		

Page	Skill	Mastered	Needs Practice
66–67	Medial Consonants		
68–70	Silent Consonants: *dge, kn, wr*		
71–73	Initial 2-Letter Consonant Blends		
74–75	Initial 3-Letter Consonant Blends		
76	Final Consonant Blends: *ft, ld, lt, nt*		
77–78	Final Consonant Blends: *mp, nd, sk, st*		
79–80	Initial Consonant Digraphs: *ch, sh, th, wh*		
81–84	Final Consonant Digraphs: *ch, sh, tch, th*		
85–86	Final Consonant Digraphs: *ck, ng, nk*		
87–88	Consonant Digraphs: *gh, ph, ff*		
90–92	Action Word Ending: *ed*		
93–97	Action Word Endings: *ed, ing*		
98–104	Action Word Endings: *es, ing, s*		
105–108	Plural Endings: *s, es*		
109–110	Plural Ending: *es*		
111–112	Comparative Endings: *er, est*		
114–115	Suffixes: *ful, y*		
116–117	Suffix: *ly*		
118–119	Suffix: *ness*		
120–121	Suffix: *able*		
122–124	Prefixes: *dis, un*		
125–127	Prefixes: *pre, re*		
128–130	Contractions with *'d, 're, 've*		
131–133	Contractions with *'ll, 'm, n't, 's*		
134–136	Compound Words		
137–138	Singular and Plural Possessives		

At Home with Phonics 141

Name

142 Core Skills

© 2004 Steck-Vaughn

Progress Chart Instructions

Each dot represents an activity page. As your child completes the activities, note it on the chart by marking the page number or placing a sticker on each dot.

At Home with Phonics 143

Photo Acknowledgements

At Home with Phonics, Grade 2
Photo Credits

©Artville, p. 104 *notebook*; ©Joe Atlas/Artville, pp. 44 *magnifying glass*, 101 *badge* 104 *magnifying glass*, 110 *binder*; Bill Burlingham, p. 129; ©Comstock, pp .44 *boy*, 47 *girl*, 84, 108, 128 *girl*, 130; ©Corbis, pp. 62, 63, 88 *mouth*; ©Corel, pp. 108 *background*, 110 *ruler, paper clips, background*; ©Digital Vision, p. 104 *girl*; courtesy Federal Bureau of Investigation, p. 44 *fingerprints*; Sharon Hoogstraten, p. 1; ©Hot Shots Photografx, pp. 82, 106 *spinner*, 108 *hand, watch*, 128 *spinner*; Allan Landau Photography, pp. 92, 106 *boy*, 116; ©Meta Tools, pp. 36, 101 *clipboard*, 112; Ken O'Donoghue, p. 3, 4; ©PhotoDisc, pp. 15, 23, 31, 34, 35, 40, 47 *background*, 68, 88 *trophy*, 99, 101 *pencil*, 104 *boys*, 120-1, 134 *watch, dog, bird, house, cup, cake, box*; ©Rubberball/PNI, p. 134 *coat*; ©Marty Snyderman/Corbis, p. 134 *fish*; ©SuperStock, p. 13; Brian Warling, *cover*.

Core Skills